Novel Writing

Novel Writing

A Writers' and Artists' Companion

**Romesh Gunesekera and
A. L. Kennedy**

Series Editors: **Carole Angier and Sally Cline**

Bloomsbury Academic
An imprint of Bloomsbury Publishing Plc

B L O O M S B U R Y
LONDON · NEW DELHI · NEW YORK · SYDNEY

Bloomsbury Academic

An imprint of Bloomsbury Publishing Plc

50 Bedford Square
London
WC1B 3DP
UK

1385 Broadway
New York
NY 10018
USA

www.bloomsbury.com

BLOOMSBURY and the Diana logo are trademarks of Bloomsbury Publishing Plc

First published 2015

British Library Cataloguing-in-Publication Data
A catalogue record for this book is available from the British Library.

ISBN: PB: 978-1-7809-3710-6
ePDF: 978-1-7809-3788-5
ePub: 978-1-7809-3826-4

Library of Congress Cataloging-in-Publication Data
A catalog record for this book is available from the Library of Congress.

Series: Writers' and Artists' Companions

Typeset by Deanta Global Publishing Services, Chennai, India
Printed and bound in India

Contents

Part 2: Tips and tales – guest contributions

Part 3: Write on

Contents

Foreword

Novel

(a foreword)

It was the middle of the night and something too bright woke me. I opened my eyes, because, what was it, an angel? A bad or good fairy? Some kind of magic being from the sort of story we never believed in even when we were kids and were meant to? Whatever it was had clearly been there shaking the covers for some time.

What? I said.

I shielded my eyes. I saw it wasn't a magic anything. It was just a bare light bulb.

Hi, it said.

(Yes, brightly).

Oh, right, I said. The light bulb moment.

Its element glowed.

Good for you, I said. Enjoy your moment. I'm off back to sleep.

No. Wait, the light bulb said.

It was the old-fashioned kind of light bulb that lights up fully immediately. They're environmentally unsound, I know, though I kind of miss the kick of them in the new slightly too-sickly slowness that flicking a switch makes happen these days.

But when I went to close my eyes to it, this one, 100-watt-bright already and no lampshade, suddenly got even more fierce and bright. It glowed right at me as if about to blow.

What? I said.

Wake up, it said.

No, I said.

Get up. I'm – ta daaaa – the start of the new novel, it said.

Yeah, I know, I said.

Write this down, it said. Ready?

Oh God, I said.

No, I really can't claim to be God, it said. Though formally – I mean, I don't speak for myself, I speak for the whole novel form here – there can be quite a lot of gloriousness, revolution, vision, prophecy, ancient story, metamorphic form, narrative tricksiness and moral and social questioning involved, and even after all that I haven't even really started to list them, the possibilities.

I don't understand how you're speaking at all, I said, since you've got no mouth and you're made of glass and metal and chemicals.

And you're supposed to be imaginative? It said.

Go away, I said.

I can't, it said.

Please, I said. I've just *finished* a novel. Leave me alone. I'm exhausted.

How can I? It said. I'm here now. I'm going to do what I do – keep waking you just before you drop off every night, and waking you in the middle of the night most nights till I'm finished, and waking you up in the morning every morning from now till God knows when telling you glorious and revolutionary and visionary and prophetic and ancient and tricksy and metamorphic and moral and social things about *me*. And of course there'll also be all the mornings when I wake you up and don't say a single thing, nothing, nothing, nothing at all.

And you're the reason I'll be reasonably poorly off for 3 years out of the next 4 years, I said.

Yes, but only if you actually spend the advance, it said.

How can I not? I have to live on something, I said. I'm lucky to have it at all. And you're going to eat everything in the house.

Anyway I don't care what *you* need, the light bulb said. *Come on.*

It hovered. It got even nearer. It was literally nearly in the bed with me, which would mean singed sheets. I shut my eyes but it was so close to me now that the light came straight through the lids and the heat in it meant danger.

I waited a bit.

When I dared to open one eye, there it still was.

It was shining as bare as the word bare at me.

Oh, all right then, I said.

Great, it said. Come on then.

Right now? I said. It's really late. We'll start tomorrow.

Never too late, it said.

It swung across the room and hung, camp and playful, menacing and welcoming, in the air above the desk.

I got up. I sighed. I crossed the room.

But this time, you, I said. I'm just letting you know. I'm not alone in this.

Not alone? It said. Don't be ridiculous. Just you and me. Nobody else. Nothing else. Otherwise you won't be able to do it.

Yep, I said. Just you and me, and my, you know, companion.

What companion? The light bulb said.

Oh, you know. Just every book I've ever read. Just every book ever written whether I've read it or not, I said.

Well, okay, it said. I can't deny you them. It's family. More the merrier.

Oh, yeah, and this book, I said. It's new. Look.

I opened a book on the desk.

When I did, and flicked through it, it was like a party had broken out there on my desk, a really lively one full of people I knew and interesting people I'd not yet met and writers I'd already read and writers I hadn't yet, brand new writers, seasoned and experienced writers, and they were all talking and arguing and agreeing and disagreeing and the glasses were clinking, the food was plentiful and the music was happening by itself behind it all.

I shut the book.

I sat in the light.

I listened. Silence.

Right, I said. Ready.

Ali Smith

Preface

In *Novel Writing*, the seventh in our Writers' & Artists' series of books on writing, we are extraordinarily lucky to have two leading contemporary novelists to share with us their deep knowledge and love of the genre.

Romesh Gunesekera and A L Kennedy begin with a lively dialogue about the novel in general – what differentiates it from the short story, how much invention makes non-fiction into fiction (even a bit, says Kennedy), whether the novel has lost the moral and social role it had in the days of Dickens (Kennedy thinks it has, Gunesekera is more optimistic), and much more.

This beginning is exactly right, since Part 1 is a debate between two writers who start from very different places, but meet somewhere in the middle. Thus, for example, Kennedy prefers a good clear plan in advance (though it may of course change), while Gunesekera finds that much can grow and evolve in the writing – including even doing a lot of the research after he's finished the first draft. On the other hand Kennedy fears things setting in stone if she reworks too much as she goes, and recommends carrying on and re-writing later; while Gunesekera says firmly that nit-picking is OK and we all do it, the problem is only knowing when to stop (after you've put in the same comma and taken it out three times, he suggests.) Kennedy has especially good advice on characters (e.g. engage especially with the ones you don't like), and Gunesekera on point of view and perspective (this, he says, is the most important decision you'll have to make.)

Part 2 is, as usual, a bumper crop of short reflections from some of the best practitioners of the genre today, including this time ten of the Granta Best of Young British Novelists 2013. Then with Part 3 we return to our two authors, with a practical guide to novel writing. Here they deal in detail with unusual ideas such as silence, distance, false starts and experimentation of every kind, as well as the more familiar nuts and bolts of grammar, punctuation, tenses and point of view. And they pass on one of their favourite pieces of writing advice of all, which comes from Flannery O'Connor: 'Every morning between 9 and 12 I go to my room and sit before a piece of paper. Many times I just sit for 3 hours with no ideas coming to me. But I know one thing: if an idea did come between 9 and 12, I am there ready for it.'

Some of our own favourite pieces of advice come from the authors of *Novel Writing* themselves. From A L Kennedy, for instance: *Be in the world and pay attention*; and from Romesh Gunesekera, that the best practice for writing is writing itself. And if you'd like to know why A L Kennedy sticks to her initials, you can find out here. Happy reading and happy writing to everyone.

Carole Angier and Sally Cline, Series editors

Part 1:
On novel writing

Reflections

What is a novel?

A dialogue between A. L. Kennedy and Romesh Gunesekera

Romesh Gunesekera: We've both been reading a lot of novels, in a concentrated period, over the last year. And many before that. So, what is a novel for you?

A. L. Kennedy: I suppose the form is about a number of relationships for me. As a reader, I'm looking for something that gives me time and depth – or, rather the illusion of time and depth – with characters, with a world, with concepts, with a mind and a voice. It's not a chat – which I suppose would be the equivalent of an Op-ed piece. It's not some kind of intense, condensed encounter – like a short story. It's a form which comes close to 'finishing the conversation' if I could paraphrase Ford Madox Ford. Word length, or themes, or plots – the kind of things that can get very formulaic when agents and editors are scared – don't really provide a satisfactory definition and that's why the form is being distorted by 'the marketplace' and it's only in areas like Sci-Fi and Fantasy that real freedom and daring seem to be allowed. For a writer, it's the long process of establishing and maintaining those relationships and building a real fiction over time that defines the novel experience. A short story feels different – more like accosting someone in a lift. A novella is exhausting – a process of maintaining the tension of a short fiction over a longer span, but not so long that characters and scenarios really kick in to assist in the way that they do with a novel. And then you have the novel – within which you are eventually collaborating in the fullest possible sense with elements that you previously created – it is the least isolated form of writing, I think. . . .

RG: I like the idea of seeing it in terms of a relationship. A novel becomes one for the reader when it develops into a relationship over time. It allows re-reading, mis-reading, forgetting, rediscovering – all those sorts of things. If the book isn't doing that, then perhaps it isn't a novel.

I was also trying to work out how one recognizes a novel. In the past there were physical indicators. With the Penguin paperback revolution a novel was easy to identify: about 160 pages of fiction between covers. After the 1970s novels became fat, a bit like when they first started out with *Don Quixote* and *Tristam Shandy*. Sometimes location tells you that this is a novel. It is there on a shelf labelled 'fiction'. But that's unreliable. Unfamiliar novels get shelved elsewhere. I remember finding novels in anthropology sections when I first started out.

ALK: I think the novel can offer the most deeply personal experience of fiction on both sides of the interaction, simply because of the time element – either the illusion of time or its actuality. Obviously, one can sit and read a novel in a day . . . but the sense is of a long journey having been undertaken and completed. And the writer has – almost always – already made their own long journey.

The recognition of the form is tricky – you know it when you see it. . . . A highly crafted novel like *Handcarved Coffins* by Truman Capote can be – due to a blend of insecurities – initially presented as journalism. James Frey's *A Million Little Pieces* was again something constructed, but put forward as truthful memoir. Now it has been repositioned as semi-fictional. I have to say, as far as that 'semi' label goes, if fiction is in the mix, then it's in the whole mix. If there's a little bit of horsemeat in your steak pie, you're unhappy about the whole pie. . . . I think the angry reaction to the bad faith in the presentation of that particular book was heartening, and the trend towards categories that mislead the reader is generally depressing. The longing for really good 'misery memoirs', often ghost-written, often very close to what one might describe as fiction . . . the 'true' war memoirs. . . . We seem to be losing the truth of 'truth' in the novel as we are in so many other areas. And meanwhile the 'truth' of fiction – the attempt to create *something* which has a core of substantial reality from the *nothing* of blended inspirations, chances, dreams, necessities, obsessions and so forth – becomes devalued or forgotten. This may be connected with the journalistic and academic desire to define all creativity as simple plagiarism from reality. It's the kind of thing that C. S. Lewis mocked and yet here we are a few decades later, expected to believe that any novel comes directly and ploddingly from the author's life. This can have a toxic effect on young writers, apart from anything else – they can see themselves as condemned to mine their intimate relationships and borrow their friends in the most parasitic and dull way. . . .

And then you have the sometimes bizarre decisions made by the world about the reader and the writer – a regional or non-Caucasian writer must be pigeonholed at once, a book by a woman must have X type of cover whether it's appropriate or not, the author and the work will be conflated in the press . . . and so on.

RG: Novels do invite games. So the play between autobiography and fiction has always been there. If it is done well it can work fabulously well, as in Naipaul's *Enigma of Arrival*, but if done badly it is dire. Sometimes playing means not telling whether it is fiction or not. But sometimes it seems okay to play it straight. Readers are not usually upset if fiction is not entirely fiction, but they would be if it claimed to be non-fiction and turns out to be fiction. It is surprising how often things are proclaimed to be what they are: X, a collection of stories, Y, a novel. Come to think of it, my first novel had a subtitle on the original hardback cover: '*Reef*, a novel'. I am not sure what my publishers thought it might be mistaken for, but by paperback time it had lost the phrase.

Richard Ford in his musings about the short story comes to the conclusion that the only sure clue that a story is a short story is if the author says it is. I guess you could use that same principle for the novel: if the writer says it is a novel, then it is one. With the caveat that sometimes even when the writer says it is not a novel, it is one.

So if anything goes and you want to write a novel, is there anything to hang on to?

ALK: Hmm. . . . I don't know if anything does go, as far as one's relationship with the reader is concerned. As a reader, I tend to get brassed off if I'm being lied to by someone I've given my time to in either direction. I think bad faith is bad faith and if you're lying it's not the best way to tell someone a story (either if you're lying about telling the truth or lying about lying). No one is going to believe that an autobiography is exhaustive, but I do expect honesty at around about Henry Greene levels, or that sense of honesty – otherwise it's just not that interesting. The illusion of honesty in what has been established as a lie would also be what I expect. As you say, the grisly dragging out of what's clearly someone else's attempt to exorcize a divorce, or an affair and so forth . . . I could do without. And there are times when I'll read something that feels somehow hammered into a plot and generally that's the lump of undigested autobiography, or the story that seemed really interesting when the author heard it. . . . Everything in any form of fiction has to have its own life as fiction, or it just doesn't fly technically and it generally leaves everyone with a bad taste in the mouth. Other than that . . . well anything goes up to a point, but basically length will define your end product as a novel. You could say a novella is a novel – lots of people do, given that the mere word 'novella' will give an editor fits – but often it won't feel like a novel to the reader – it will be a bit more intense and yet a bit less substantial. You could try to parlay a long short story of Chekhovian proportions into a novella and then bump it up to a novel, but you'd need a considerable force of personality or a massive reputation that would mean everyone would put up with your deathless prose arriving in a rather light portion. There's something about the way we take in stories, I would guess, that means we define a novel as something that takes time and commitment in a way that nothing else does. Within that form, it's relatively forgiving of saggy patches or ludicrous endings, or bizarre plots, or sheer flights of fancy. But size matters.

Personally, I know I'm having an idea which relates to a novel (and the other ideas that will interact with it and give rise to a novel) because I am overwhelmed by a sudden rush of terror. Finding the starting point of a short story is like swimming and seeing a turtle in the water with you. For a novel it's like swimming and looking over your shoulder at a speeding dorsal fin – it might be a dolphin, but you somehow doubt it. And even dolphins don't always play nice.

RG: It does need to fly. Or at least float. I am very conscious when writing a novel (more than with a short story) that I am trying to build something impossible, like an aircraft. How could it possibly fly when it is made of things heavier than air? And then somehow you try and hope and pray and run with it until suddenly it takes to the air. Maybe briefly before gravity pulls. But luckily with a novel the material is lighter than air: words.

You could also put it in terms of ships rather than aircraft. I heard Richard Ford say the other day that when you write a novel you feel you have made a ship looking for somewhere to sink. So, bring on the dolphins. Or the angels.

ALK: Oddly, at some point when I'm kicking off to start a novel, I always think of Ahab on his ship. Once the crew are aboard and too far from shore to swim home, he reveals his objective and swears them to it and makes them a new religion and on they all go to their certain doom. . . . It always reminds me of the novel. Hopefully, the novel's crew are happy to be there – the fictional people have wanted to be involved and the cabins and fittings are to their liking – the non-fictional reader can be beguiled into not jumping ship and finding my set of obsessions entertaining, or at least tolerable, and the sea is below and the sky is above and not vice versa. . . . Hopefully.

It is an impossible form or would be if it were translated into another medium. If you were to stage or film the novel, for example, the cast would have to be perfect, the direction flawless, the script ideal, as with the weather, the setting, the photography, the editing, the mise-en-scène and so forth. If you think of the difficulty of staging something like *King Lear* – all the technical demands that get put into a production and how rarely something of that scale completely succeeds . . . it's a great mercy that the novel is entirely virtual. In the author's mind and in that of the reader, all these elements can – potentially – be ideal or as near to ideal as we need them to be.

RG: I love the idea of Ahab there. And so right that he should be there. C. L. R. James said that Ahab is one of the last great new fictional characters created. Meaning a completely new personality type. Like Hamlet. A rare thing. And yes, I recognize that feeling of setting the stage, getting everything ready and hoping the tank is full. And how exhilarating to promise doom and at the very last moment find the reprieve: you reach the end and you come up for air.

Ahab also makes me wonder about control. One of the things that I marvel at in a good novel is the control in it, and clearly as a writer you do control the writing. Characters don't really start typing the words, but at the same time there is a shape in the novel, or the story, that controls the whole thing. And as a writer one is constantly trying to find it. What you are trying to get to in the writing is something that cannot but be what it is and all the rewriting, the revisions and the changes are trying to get it into the shape that makes it exactly what it is. At one level it seems everything has to be perfect, otherwise the boat sinks. And yet, I can also understand how a great novel can have big flaws. I suppose it is a bit like the perfect liner that hits the iceberg and sinks and the Kon-Tiki that keeps on sailing despite water lapping up between the odd logs of the raft. In *Moby Dick*, who is in charge? Ahab? Ishmail? The great white whale? Melville? The reader? The reader is the one who can open or close the book. But in a good novel maybe the reader can't close the book. Someone in there might keep knocking on the door of the reader's imagination: open up, open up. Read, read. Finish the book! As a writer what you want is that same call: write, write, finish the book!

ALK: By the end of the novel, there is a sense of the elements and personalities and psychologies having made certain things impossible to avoid, or highly likely, and of having ruled out many, many other paths. That does seem to make the last stages of the novel much more relaxing in a way. It's anxiety-provoking, because you're near the completion of what might have been a waste of years. . . . But you're also close to being off the hook, having a sleep without Ahab and the whale intruding upon your dreams, and you're being assisted by decisions you've made earlier.

Having taken a break from writing prose fiction for quite a while last year, I have to say that I am appreciating the sheer physical comfort and, I suppose, the kind of mental calm that comes from simply focusing on the novel, the characters and the plot progression. It all feels especially soothing this time around – even though I am at the beginning of the process, where very few decisions have been made and there are days when it can feel like a slog.

RG: Do you think novelists have always had these feelings: the anxieties at the beginning, the delicious delusions in the middle, and the calm before the inevitable end? Or is it different now with wider readerships, the discussions about books, the connection writers have with audiences and readers, and the time scale in which things happen? I wonder how it felt for a writer like Laurence Sterne playing with *Tristram Shandy*, or Defoe or the Brontës. What would have been their sense of the thread that links writers, or the novel, through the ages? Would it be the heady sense of doing something never done before, that Samuel Beckett or William Burroughs or Gertrude Stein might have felt? Can anyone feel that now?

ALK: One would hope that it's still possible to feel there could be something new we could offer – either very well crafted and slyly experimental, like Richard Ford's *Canada*, or equally crafted but wildly expressive and ambitious like Will Self's *Umbrella*. I think that in the United Kingdom there are now so many huge divisions between different cultures, regions and generations that there is a great deal of scope for the novel to open up very new worlds to readers. . . . Whether the publishing industry can actually get these novels to readers or recognize something outside the safe bets would be another question.

In a way, I can feel nostalgic for the days when novelists were hyper-engaged and classified themselves as Realists, Modernists, Magic Realists. . . . I don't find classifications that useful myself, but the idea that the novel was at the heart of cultural developments from the time that mass reading became a reality is very exciting. We seem to have lost much of the philosophical underpinning and the confidence of the form – it's no longer expected to offer any kind of moral reformation – as all kinds of people, including Robert Louis Stevenson, assumed it should, after centuries of art having some kind of elevating purpose. The novel is not looked on as a major catalyst of social or political change, or as a witness in the way that Charles Dickens, or Alan Sillitoe, Upton Sinclair, Émile Zola, John Steinbeck, or someone like João Ubaldo Ribeiro or Juan Perucho might have thought, in their various ways. As nothing is forbidden and everything is permitted, there can be nothing as shocking and subversive as de Sade's *Justine* – although a great deal that's equally as laughable. Voltaire or Swift going to the novel to examine their world with deep satire, Samuel Madden and Cyrano de Bergerac breaking free from their own times and places to look back at them critically – Cyrano using space travel to gain perspective on seventeenth-century France and Madden writing *Memoirs of the Twentieth Century* while inhabiting eighteenth-century Ireland. . . . These days, do we expect the novel to be that hard-hitting, that vital, that inventive? At the moment, it can sometimes seem that Sci-Fi is the one area where there still are signs of life – somehow the literary novel has ceded a great deal of territory to the blandness of marketing departments, Hollywood formulae, boil-in-the-bag creative writing courses and low expectations. Novels which have battled their way through the current publishing scene in the United Kingdom and the United States often seem to be romances in the very smallest sense. I know there are other kinds of books out there, but we seem unable to reach them, and they us. Many authors are working – as so many, particularly female writers, did in the nineteenth century – with little hope of ever being read.

RG: I think it is interesting to distinguish the excitement of innovation in the novel from the excitement of the novel as a catalyst for wider social change. The scope and effect of both are different from what they were in the past. I suspect that to have the same far-reaching effect in the cultural and artistic sphere, one may need to look at the new digital media being explored by many writers. Probably a hybrid art form. The likelihood of a modern novel having the sort of social impact that novels had in the nineteenth century may seem unlikely but I don't think it should be discounted. The impact may not be as obvious as in the days of Dickens, Zola or Sinclair, but a novel may still open eyes, sensitize people or change values. I think even the growth of interest in fiction and fiction writing, which in turn feeds a growing publishing and literary culture, as can be seen in some parts of the world, does change societies. Not in the sense of legislation as it was in the past, but actually even that too if one thinks in terms of censorship, freedom of expression and so on. So you might see a development of wider social effects from Dickens, Zola and Sinclair, for example, to Solzhenitsyn and Klima et al, and then onto the next stage. Within the art of the novel, the development would be different: the great changes heralded by the Modernists or the Magic Realists, or the individual writers who affect the way that new writers approach the novel: Joyce, Woolf, Becket, Faulkner, Forster . . . on to Márquez, Kundera, Rushdie and so on. Perhaps the difference now is that one can pick and choose one's tradition from a wider range and with less fuss than before.

If we bring it back to the practicalities, are these thoughts about the novel and what it means best considered before you write a novel, or after you have finished one or while you are doing it?

ALK: I think outside the UK/US literary culture – which is kind of destroying itself and has really lost its way in many areas – there is probably more potential for the novel. Really, it's a thing of faith – we have to believe in it before we can write it, and if the culture around us believes in it, then it can change lives, inside and out. And if the culture buries it alive, it's harder for it to have an impact or even reach a reader. Which is sad, because it's such a lovely form. Hopefully, new technologies will assist the transmission of novels along with everything else – although good work will get lost in the electronic ocean of less-good work and, with each innovation, there seems to be more and more pressure for authors to pay for being published, to give work away, to develop a life where they write, but never earn a living by writing. That's not necessarily a disaster, but it makes it hard if you want to write full-time and are not independently wealthy. Obviously, around the world, writing for a living is a much rarer phenomenon . . . and people get by. Writers still write, even when they know they may be imprisoned or executed for doing so – we can't be stopped. It's simply frustrating when we are unnecessarily delayed and some voices fade through lack of support.

Getting to your question – I don't personally find consideration of categories imposed by literary criticism all that useful when I think of my work, never mind when I'm planning it. I deal with a fair number of new writers and creative writing students – as you do – and I'm aware of how easily waylaid intelligent young people can be by the language and thought patterns of literary criticism. It's relatively easy to develop the thesis for a potential novel, to be intellectually intrigued by this or that theory but I think that to sustain a novel, you need a much deeper connection to your material and the novel as a beast unique to you. A novel may be classified in all kinds of ways, compared to all kinds of other work – and I know that mine have been rattled about and filed away in terms that I found bizarre. I've been told I'm heavily-influenced by people I've never read and totally committed to philosophies in which I have little interest – that whole game has nothing much to do with putting words on paper so that someone else will believe them – that's much nearer life and death. I don't think anyone would write at all costs if writing were just a game for undergraduates to analyse according to terms provided beforehand.

What kind of things do you find you talk about with young writers? I tend to spend a lot of time on nuts-and-bolts attention to syllables – a level at which people get tired and shaky quite fast – and looking at overall development of projects from a distance, getting the overview – which also seems hard when you're 'in' a book. The people who turn up with great ideas about relating themselves to the European literary tradition on XXXX, or whatever, tend to have great difficulty in actually putting words on paper, or making them live. A novel isn't a theory. Although it's fiction, perhaps because it's fiction – it has to be a fact. When you've finished it, the theories go away – it should be there. A fact.

RG: I agree with a lot of those points. Too often new writers try too hard to put something they are keen on (an idea, a theory, an experience) into a novel which unfortunately the novel does not want. It has its own shape and sometimes the writer's dearest thoughts have no place in it.

The discussions I have with students and aspiring novelists are invariably about either (a) how to start, or (b) how to keep going. Most of what we have in this book is about those two questions. Theory and literary criticism have hardly any place, although I try to bring in some talk about other novels so that one can appreciate what else has been written and how it has been done. Most of the time I try to look into the details of a sentence and then at the overall book in terms of its structure. When you are starting a book, and when you trying to keep going on, I think it helps to know something about the structure you are aiming for: big or small, something in parts, something uninterrupted. But it needs to be something that can change. It is just a way of getting in motion. Some people like getting in the car and starting to drive and then deciding where they want to get to depending on the traffic, etc; others don't want to open the door, let alone start the engine, without deciding their destination, and once decided will not waver even if it takes a lifetime to get there. The choice is between wanting to write novels and wanting to write one particular novel – that one, and no other. What happens, I guess, is something in between. And that's when it is worth thinking of how other writers have done it. I am not sure what Virginia Woolf expected to produce when she first started on *To the Lighthouse*, but we have a good idea of what Mary Shelley was aiming at with *Frankenstein*. Or take the journey we go on with Don DeLillo and compare it to the one we would take with Chinua Achebe.

ALK: There is always this difficulty, when working with others, that one writer just doesn't think like another – and you're hoping a new writer will become more and more themselves and not a copy of anyone else and yet one can only give guidance or advice using one's own particular way of thinking as a starting point. . . . When a writer begins to write, or begins a specific project, they may have ideas about what will keep them going, or how to prepare or how to keep on, that aren't at all helpful. Writing is a great way to find out how you think and develop how you think, but that takes time. Meanwhile, mistakes will be made. In fact, they're essential because they're so deeply educational. It's quite hard to emphasize the importance of failure and missteps and being left to work things out and grow, when the writing culture in the United Kingdom and the United States – and it's beginning to be like this in Europe too – is so focused on a quite rigid model with learning outcomes expected within months, and courses and exercises and workshops, really a lot of things that get in the way of the writing. I suspect a one-year MA course or something like that would have done me no end of harm when I was starting out – although that's just speaking for myself. And some of the software out there that purports to support writing is frankly criminal.

I think there's a lot to be said for a bit of on-going self-knowledge and sensible simplicity. I would hope those would give one the best chance of success.

The novel – what I wish I'd known before I started

A. L. Kennedy

Creative worrying

I once heard someone ask a friend of mine who is now successful in one of the arts what he would have said to himself in his younger days, what advice his inexperienced self might have most needed. Rather than laying down the law about agents, contracts, training, clean living or perhaps networking, he thought for a bit and then suggested he could usefully have told himself that he needn't worry so much. This might have seemed impractical as an example to others, or even smug – a man who had made it, reassuring himself that he was always going to have made it – but then he went on to elaborate, to mention all those mornings when he'd woken up sick with fear and been besieged by his apparently hopeless situation. He'd had the time to realize how much effort he'd poured into being pointlessly terrified.

I found myself agreeing. I too had ground away at my stamina in sleepless nights and uneasy dawns just when I needed vast amounts of energy to discover how I might live up to the demands of a highly exacting vocation. Not to mention actually getting down to work. I knew I loved writing. I fretted that it didn't love me back, that I would run out of ideas, that the ideas I had were no use, that no one would want to read me, that I would never make a living, that I was kidding myself (I wasn't absolutely sure in what way), that I would never get any better, that I didn't understand 'the business', that I didn't look or sound or (I was guessing) *feel* like any of the writers that I read about in magazine profiles, or biographies or saw on TV. I had very little money, I was cold a good deal of the time, I had a dead-end nearly-job and a nastily undefined future. I desperately needed mental clarity, self-assurance and the ability to rest and yet . . . I worried. Instead of relaxing when I could, I worried. Instead of planning sanely, I worried. Instead of using my imagination to build things for other people to read, I worried.

I was wasting my time.

Deeply, deeply, I was wasting my time.

And that day when I realized – having only written short stories hitherto – that my latest idea could only be expressed in novel form? Panic attack. Sheer horror. I could feel my mind squirming in protest and only being prevented from leaving by my implacable skull.

Which was unhelpful.

The first thing I wish I'd known when embarking upon a novel was that worrying should be strenuously and constantly controlled. It can be a friend or an enemy and we have the power to decide which. I'm not saying that you won't, or shouldn't, worry when you're starting out on a novel. You may well be at the beginning of your career and you are certainly at the start of a process which could take months, if not years, one with no guaranteed triumph at its conclusion. If you ever reach its conclusion. You may already have experience of failing to write a short story, or an article – now it seems possible that you'll *fail to produce a whole novel*, that you'll pit yourself against what is held to be prose's pre-eminent form and then blow it. And if you've got an agent, even an editor, if you've managed to wheedle an advance out of some magnificently reckless publishing house . . . it just gets worse.

The fear can be slowly toxic, or instantly paralysing: generating blurry, non-committal prose or complete silence. So clearly there's a power in worry. If you care about something, you worry. And I would hope, for your sake, that you care about your writing. How, then, do we harness that care, that worry?

I feel that it's useful to regard worries as reminders to stay safe, as moments when we've let our hand slip too near some flame or other and should move ourselves to a place of safety, rather than being roasted to the bone.

For example – there's no point expecting writing to love us the way we love it. How could it possibly love us? It's an it. If we're looking for our efforts to be reciprocated, then probably we should focus on making those efforts as effective as possible. Then there's an outside chance that someone may read us and like what we've done, that we'll be able to earn more money and therefore more time and therefore do more writing. And the novel – given publishing's current preferences – is still the form they expect fiction authors to produce if they want to be commercially viable.

We can practice discounting fake fears. We aren't, for example, going to run out of ideas. No one does unless they develop a degenerative disease, or a severe head injury, and even then. . . .

And when the fake fear has gone, we can address legitimate concerns. What about those ideas we're never going to run out of? Novels – even apparently simple and slight novels – are huge and hungry for anything we can offer. It's our job to train ourselves to assess, support, develop and then employ our ideas. That takes practice, so we need to start now. If we fear our ideas aren't good enough, that our writing isn't good enough, that our words, phrases, sentences and paragraphs aren't good enough then we should make them better. If our words are going to form a novel, to carry the reader on that long journey, then we need to make sure our preparations are helpful and that our focus and concentration stay at reasonable levels throughout the progress of the work.

Our horror of being not good enough is a wonderful friend. It encourages us to try harder, which means we can learn. It makes us practice what we do until we are better at it and then practice again until we are better yet and on and on. This is particularly important with a novel – they take so bloody long to produce that we should try to ensure that they educate us, that they help us to be the author that can write them in the best possible way. Our horror – converted to a kind of practical pressure to perform – can give us and our novels a life of positive development and change across all the forms. Why would that be a cause for concern?

We can kid ourselves in our craft by thinking that we won't have to put the hours in. We can imagine that engaging in displacement activities – like scaring ourselves, playing aimlessly with our cast, shifting scenes about with no real grasp of why – will achieve something. But we'd be wrong.

I was certainly wrong. My early fretting made me feel fastidious and wise. If I'd spent more time making plans and forestalling disaster, rather than being transfixed by its approach, I would have been able to put all my strength into actually writing my novel. Moving beyond my love for what I was doing, I had to learn to commit to the pursuit of perfection without taking it personally. A bad book would still be a bad book, even if I loved it ever so much. I had to start really writing – not simply making up people, places and things, playing make-believe. I had to learn how to set my available elements into structures, how to allow them to act upon each other, how to make them into something which a reader might love. The novel demands a commitment from the reader, time and effort – one way or another, it has to reward them for that or they simply won't stick around. Writers can maintain all kinds of high-flown theories about what we believe the novel to be – and all kinds of highly intellectual reasons for avoiding this or that area we feel we can't manage. But the readers don't have to agree with us. They owe us nothing – we owe them everything. If we are full of wild ideas and edgy schemes, we have to make them readable. Even if we are being doggedly conventional, we still have to connect with that person other than ourselves who has to read us, who will help us earn enough money to have time to write more. . . .

If you're troubled by the thought of contracts, finding an agent or placing your material, then look at *The Writer's Handbook*, *The Writers' and Artists' Yearbook* or the myriad of other sources in print and online, contact published writers or writers in residence, attend readings and other literary events. Study the novel form as you would a lover: stalk it, adore it, be impatient with it, *know* it.

And let your worries keep you personally and professionally safe. If something doesn't feel right, don't panic – try and identify the problem area. If you don't like the way your agent is reacting to your material, maybe you really do have to bite the bullet and go elsewhere. If you feel your voice is being compromised, maybe you're wrong and everyone else is right, maybe you should be good child and take what seems an ill-fitting opportunity. Or maybe you should defend yourself, try fighting your corner, even walk away. The individuality of your writing is all you have. Your agent and your editor are servants of your voice – as are you. In reality, you'll feel as if you're working for them. In reality, you are. But if you don't care for your voice, it won't be there for you quite as strongly the next time you need it. My first editorial experience (for a collection of short stories) involved being swamped by the opinions of a dozen reader's reports – it was a uselessly appalling and contradictory din which I should have been spared. My first novel had the attentions of a professional editor at the height of his powers – gentle questions, interesting suggestions and plenty of time to mend what I thought I needed to and move on sounding more like myself. I would wish you the same, although in these days of unthinking commercial pressure, tiny advances and semi-constant rejection, you may not be so lucky. Publishing in the United Kingdom (and many other countries) has its own fear-related problems and we all, as writers, have to pay the price for them.

But worrying about 'the business' and its tottering health is pointless – it's the intellectual equivalent of watching a once-glorious companion shoot themselves to death from the feet up. Address what you do have a chance of changing for the better. Keep a grip on your chosen market, read widely and deeply, research which editors and agents might like your material. But mainly write. That effortless prose you read in the writers you admire, the smooth roll of lyricism that makes you forget everything? It has its roots in total effort and forgetting nothing – the writer works, so the reader doesn't notice when they have to. One word after another, you can make yourself into the writer that you and only you can be, the exalted person that may at some point seem impressive and certain across multiple media platforms. The size and complexity of the novel, its long-term exposure to character, its demands on your stamina and style – they can all teach you as no course, or workshops, or tutor ever will. On the good days you can think of it as being a free MA degree. If I'd known how much I was learning as I wrote my first novel I would have been in despair far less often. But at that point I had so much to learn. . . . My shortcomings were hypnotizingly obvious and distracting. In time, and after a number of novels, they have become a little quieter.

I wish I had known earlier that I can nod to my concerns when they appear and try to understand what they're telling me, what I can improve. If they're just annoying, I can tell them to go. I can train them to leave relatively obediently. We work with our minds and we can train them to help us, not get in our way. I wish I had started earlier in the habit of accepting and cultivating the useful thoughts and bumping aside the obstructions and white noise.

Message from Delphi

The exhortation 'Know Thyself' is often attributed to the oracle at Delphi. It was one of the Delphic maxims they actually bothered to carve into Apollo's temple, a proverb so popular and useful that it was deemed to be heaven-sent. According to Plato, Socrates thought it to be an important principle in education. For what it's worth, I agree. And, in the context of the novel, it's essential.

I wish I'd known, as I started to write, how useful it was to actively inventory my skills and weaknesses, the ways I work well, the most effective ways I can motivate myself, the activities I would take to and those which would crush my soul, the environments that support me best, the inspirations that would feed me most sustainingly. It would have saved so much time. Setting out before the first novel, it would have been massively helpful to understand what really, truly interested me, what angers I had that were inarticulate and which would therefore fire randomly, tearing apart bits of the text, what parts of writing scared me so much I would avoid them . . . all the inventory of booby traps and pitfalls that would sabotage me as I struggled along.

I wish someone had told me that my preparations to make myself feel comfortable before I switched on and stared at the green of the screen (this was back in the days of the Amstrad) were worthwhile as an idea but overly ornate. Mainly I needed the basics: a comfortable chair, good light, a non-crippling keyboard, decent heating and music to cover the noise from the neighbours. I tried my best on all fronts but – especially while writing novels, running that marathon, attempting the hold things together as I staggered forward – I never got into the habit of taking sane, regular breaks. A decade later the stress injuries and back problems began. To be fair, many people did tell me that the human body isn't designed to type for hours on end. Their worries didn't worry me and I ignored them.

I wish someone had told me to cut out that first novel's authorial intrusions, small and large, because the book wasn't about me and there was no need for me to butt in with segments about writing, or passages of supposedly writerly crafting, just to make sure the reader knew I was around. Proper prose always, in every syllable, lets the reader know the writer is around, but the relationship isn't forced. Your reader is busy watching the play – they don't need you bellowing in their ear every 10 minutes with 'Hey, we're in the Olivier. Look at the nice purple seats! And this is me! Me being Hamlet! Hamlet! But ME!' Many writers have their own versions of this tick and, in pretty much every case, we have a lot of rewriting to do as a result. This is the stuff you needn't have bothered with – for one thing, the reader is used to the novel as a form, it isn't new and wonderful to them, not in the utterly narcissistic way it can be to the new novelist. So this is what you have to cut. Almost always. It's the kind of surgery that hurts the ego, but the offending material disappears as easily as pulling your hand out of water because it has nothing to do with your book.

Back to Delphi – Apollo is a useful god, a useful metaphor to link with writing. He was associated with ecstasy, song and the arts, with illumination and prophecy. He was complicated, too: a god of healing and plague, protection and destruction, of hunting, exorcism and ambiguity. It can be slightly alarming to really examine ourselves: the passions and obsessions, the areas of laziness, the self-centred anxieties, the lack of skills, the strange areas of interest, whether we compete more with others or with ourselves, our eccentricities, the natural grain of our voices, the ways in which we are growing and changing. But that kind of taking stock is the most efficient way to turn ourselves into the best writers we can be at the moment, and to face the mountain of the novel at the stage when our only possible view involves peering dumbly upwards. We can pick ourselves to pieces by over-thinking, over-exploring who this writer is who's about to scramble up the first scree slopes and probably head for that ill-defined glacier over there. . . . But generally what we think might be a plague will actually heal us and protect us from crumbling in the face of inevitable setbacks. If we know who we are, we know how to look after ourselves. We understand our particular geography of senses and beliefs and can therefore welcome the reader into them effectively. We can deal with writing's long periods without publication, short deadlines, bizarre editing, computer failures, domestic intrusions and so forth. We can deal with the novel's sudden dead-ends, the intrusion of life into our carefully laid timetables, the collapse of previously convincing characters, the technical experiments that end up in pieces, the periods of arid doubt, the periods of intoxicating certainty. When we know ourselves in the manner of a supportive and fair friend, we can go about our business effectively – sing our songs, illuminate what we wish to and render our ecstasy articulate.

And our novel must be known, too. It will accompany us through perhaps years of hints and clues and then more formal preparations, or it may appear in an urgent mass. Including the editorial processes, even the fastest writers among us will work on a novel for more than year, at the least for more than a year. . . . We have to know it. We have to see why a reader would spend days or weeks with it, why they might return to it, and be able to enhance that kind of comradeship between what we have made and the human beings who will receive it.

But I didn't know my first novel well enough before I set out to write it and – in more than 25 years of working with other writers – I have only met two people who actually managed to over-prepare for their novels. (They had, in fact, transferred all their efforts into preparing for their novels and were never going to write them – writing them would have ended all their fun. When the novel is about other people having fun . . .) I set off with far too little knowledge of who I was writing about, what needed to happen to them, what I was really addressing in my text and what order would best serve my flows of information. I stalled at around 100 pages in when my subconscious refused to let me wander blindly on with – still – only a horrifyingly vague idea of where I was going. I rewrote heavily and learnt from that. I asked myself more and more questions and learnt from them. I began to uncover the true deep structure of what I was doing, without which any themes, vocabularies, dictionaries of imagery and atmosphere simply lie on the surface of the narrative like glitter on a poorly-crafted Christmas card. I was lucky enough to be able to move on. (Not that I'm saying my first novel turned out to be any kind of masterpiece.)

Many writers hit a wall at around the 100-page point and don't go any further. I'd rather not run that kind of risk now. I think it's easier to wait a little bit longer than you think you need to and really test your ideas. You won't find they fall apart in your hands, if you question them – your scrutiny will allow some threads to flourish and weed out the non-starters. This exploration before writing is part of what trains our minds to serve us better, assess ideas more acutely.

A novel is, as I've said, a long journey for both reader and writer – we need to be sure we have a good deal of what we'll need to carry with us when we set out. Remember that we're constructing the landscape as we go – and the company you keep. Remember that the reader has to be able to follow us and believe in whomever they meet. That will take preparation. And knowing ourselves – how we understand people, how we view the world, how we maintain our own interest – that can be of enormous help.

I also rewrote my first novel far too much at exactly the wrong stage. I fiddled with sentences almost endlessly as the first draft was rolling out and yet I was unaware of the larger pulses and over-arching concerns that might guide me. So I worked very slowly and laboriously but to very little end and, meanwhile, ended up knowing much of the book off by heart through sheer repetition. This made it tricky to rework sentences which seemed 'right' simply because they were as familiar as my home address. I should have moved forward faster and then rewritten when I could do so with a purpose. The twiddling was a kind of practice in my craft, but at a low level – like whittling under the doorpost of a timber barn with fatally loosened joists. I should have been looking elsewhere.

Appreciating one's material as a whole is something that takes practice and something you may not even know you need to practice. Moving whole chapters around in order to improve the book's performance, even replacing sections completely . . . that can seem scary. (And when I started out that kind of alteration was technically quite difficult.) But it's actually educational and empowering, once you know why you're repositioning or replacing something. And now we have computers up to the job, you can save the previous version, toy with the latest one . . . in fact, there's a great temptation to allow this kind of electronic fun to become another time-eater, along with emailing, tweeting and talking to your loved ones.

If you know your book, it will almost seem to look into you, to take your nature into account as another limiting and inspiring factor within the narrative. And if you know yourself this becomes easy to achieve and even to enjoy. Your novel isn't you. That would tend to create something ungenerous, small-minded, or childish. But your novel is *of* you. That can create something fascinating for all concerned.

A solitary vocation

I wish I'd understood what this really meant. Novel writing is very rarely collaborative and, in a fairly isolating profession, the long-term demands of the novel are particularly isolating. If you're working while you try to write one, it can seem that you'll never have enough time to complete it properly, or to get a rest from one kind of work or another. If you have a family, or a partner, you may feel that your personal life with real human beings and your personal life of the mind are in conflict to a greater or lesser degree. You may even encounter difficulties when you find yourself free to do nothing but complete your opus after receiving an advance, a grant, a fellowship, or the fruits of a lottery win. (The lottery win would be the most likely.)

I was writing my first novel while holding down a more than full-time job. My lack of planning and knowledge meant that I couldn't make the best use of what little time I had. I didn't understand how to look after myself when I was tired, or how to be brave enough to – say – spend a bus journey asking questions around a particular incident and testing its utility. And I got into the habit of writing when I should have been resting and cutting out interactions with the other areas of my life because I had so little time to get that novel finished. This tended to make the process both fragmented and joyless and part of my rewriting had to try and re-introduce at least some sense of pleasure and a degree of coherence.

It took me a long time to realize that time spent with other people and doing other things is important within the writing process. A writing life without space for pleasures becomes a prison and, although people can write well in prison they would generally prefer to create while at liberty. In the long term, treating others as appendices to our careers means they don't stay around long and we lose what they might give us, along with any sense of how pleasant it can be to give pleasure in ways that are not only papery. This robs our writing as well as ourselves. Writers don't make wonderful partners, but we don't have to be dreadful ones, either. We can incorporate love and fun and inspiration into our lives and our work.

The idea that, once I was freed from my paying job, I would do nothing but write was partly fuelled by a real love of what I now do for a living – actually being a writer and nothing but. It's a great idea. But it's not true. Writing fully-crafted prose is immensely tiring and demanding – we do generally need breaks and periods of restoration. I took me a very long time to make space for these and not to ruin hours staring at blank screens when I was stuck and feeling guilty about being stuck. If I think of the moments when I became blissfully aware of solutions to problems, pathways forwards, was suddenly granted insights into impenetrable areas, I find they have happened while I was taking a walk, or had sneaked off to the movies, when I had grudgingly agreed to spend time with friends, or was writing something to someone I loved. In short: when I wasn't writing.

The joy of not writing

As time has gone on, I have come to love writing more and more and to find the novel increasingly fascinating as a form. I am fortunate in this, because many of my mistakes could well have left me bewildered, embittered and unable to write at all, never mind attempting what we might call long-distance prose. I have been able, within the field of literary fiction, to be very free in what I do and to make my writing an expression of who I am and how I live. It is also true that who I am and how I live are expressions of how I write. Anything we do over and over again changes us, perhaps more than we change it. I would hope that the changes continue to be largely positive and exciting. I believe that is possible for any writer, and those I have come to admire most all share – among other qualities – a kind of persistent astonishment in their prose. As they age, their experience helps them, while their minds appear to grow younger, more engaged, more curious, more alive.

Whenever a mature writer announces the death of the novel it saddens me, partly because it's embarrassing when someone voluntarily makes a fool of themselves in public. But mainly I am distressed because it means that the joy has gone out of the novel for them – their novel has died, the form has kept on living and changing and they haven't found a response, the exhilarating present tense discovery of the novel has stopped happening for them and they've decided it won't return. It's less a statement of fact, more a confession of outrage and grief.

And yet, at its very start, the miracle of the novel will come and find us, apparently without our help. We never quite need to take the first step – only those that follow. We need to seek it out, but only once we know it's there, somewhere, infuriatingly somewhere. The search can be exhausting, but it makes us fit for purpose. The rewards will be unpredictable, but beyond what we can imagine. Beyond what we can imagine yet.

Writing my first novel

Romesh Gunesekera

> **❝** *Writing is swimming under water and holding your breath.* **❞**
>
> F. Scott Fitzgerald

Twenty years ago when I came up for air, after what seemed like years of writing, I found the first draft of my first novel done. I didn't know how it had happened. I still don't know for sure. A sketchy journal entry indicates that I had started only 9 months earlier, the day my first book, a collection of stories, *Monkfish Moon*, left my hands. All I had written in the diary – one notebook covering about 10 years – was 'a line here, a line there, started the novel. . . .' Then some hasty notes on life in London in the early 1990s: job worries, the recession, public sector cuts, children's schooling, iron-clad politicians clunking about like mechanical warriors and bombs. I did not think I needed to note anything else down. Or I didn't have the time. I know I was writing the novel in every spare moment I had, living in London, travelling abroad for work to China and beyond. I remember writing on the tube, underground below Eros – grabbing a few minutes between changing from the Piccadilly Line to the Bakerloo – in my lunch hour in a library or a park in Westminster, in an airport, in a hotel in Beijing, in bed, in the bath, in my head. A line here, a line there. All I knew was that for my novel to be done, I had to write it sentence by sentence, word by word, day by day. It seemed achingly slow, with little to show for any one day. I felt I was swimming in a sea of treacle, taking a breath between every stroke, not knowing if I was moving forward, or treading water or sinking. Only hoping that at some point I would discover that I was a little to closer to wherever it was I was going.

After about 6 months, I began to see the end of the story, and then there was a sense of urgency to reach it before it slipped away. At the end of the ninth month, much to my relief I found I had a story. It was hard to believe that those three or four sentences a day, the occasional page or two on a headily productive day, could have accumulated into a pile of pages – although admittedly a very small pile. It was a short novel, but it had more pages than I expected. Then it took another 9 months to get a feel for the true shape of it and rewrite the book, rewrite some parts again and again and find a perspective that worked. But that turned out to be my quickest rewrite – until now, when again I seem to have changed stroke and done a book, rewrites and all, in 2 years.

Easter 1994, 2 years after I had started the book, another rare diary note. 'Completed final proofs of *Reef*'. I had used everything around me to reach the end. It was swimming where suddenly the tide, the current, the push and pull of the water, everything seemed to help. The story pulled in everything around me: the neon lights of London, late in the century, the clam shells and seaweed on a beach in Scotland from the summer before, the yellow glow of the Star ferry in Hong Kong. Everything I had seen or felt or thought seemed to have to found a place on the page. Then finally, the day came when the book was scheduled to go to the printers. (I had editorial feedback on the way, more on that later. . . .) I called up my editor at the last minute and said 'I'd like to change one more word: "mob" to "mobs" on page x'. Or maybe the word was 'crowd'. I can't find the page now, but it was the last change at the very last moment. A final turn in some complicated mechanism that would then settle everything in its proper place and open the door to a new world. There was an explosion at the other end: 'But you've had all these months to decide. Why now? It's too late.' I retreated. 'Never mind,' I said. 'It's okay.' I had learnt something from my narrator in the book – Triton. How to survive in a changeable world. 'Mob' is right, I decided. It is fine. The book will be fine. I looked at the page again. The words had fallen into place. There was nothing more to do.

But how did I ever get to that point? What happened?

Reading first

As a young boy I was a reader and a day-dreamer. The first inkling of wanting to be a writer came from mouthing the lyrics of 'Paperback Writer', but that was because I was intoxicated by the words not the idea. Like every youngster I really wanted to be the hero in the book I was reading, or else in a rock and roll band. To be a writer was, for me at that age, to be a writer of songs, of lyrics.

What turned me on to writing pages was discovering Alan Ginsberg and the Beats a few years later. I must have been 15. They had produced books unlike anything I had seen before. The odd square shape of a City Lights book itself and then the wild words going everywhere but straight. I had grown up addicted to stories, but writers until that point had only ever been ciphers before: a signboard only indicating the type of stories contained between the covers. A brand, you might say, nothing more. Zane Grey, Alastair McLean, Ian Fleming and Leslie Charteris gave me a taste for something that I could not do without, but I didn't know who they were. Neither did I care. I only wanted a story to be lost in. And then came Ginsberg and Kerouac and a gang of outlandish writers who burst open their books and waded in proclaiming themselves as poets and writers, the authors of their destiny. The idea of writing exploded in my hands.

I read snatches of *Howl* and reams of Kerouac and had the mad idea that if I could type I could write. So I snuck my father's dusty typewriter into my room and started bashing the words out. The idea was to fill the page for prose and make uneven long lines for poetry, and always make a lot of noise in the process. I quickly realized that the typewriter, not the piano, was the instrument of my choice. And while a musician had to practice, the writer did the real thing straight off. That's what I thought then. Wrong, but immensely helpful, like all the many mistakes in a life of writing. I wrote for myself, to put into words thoughts that I did not know I had, and to entertain a few friends who'd want a line or two to read when their dodgy cassettes of the Grateful Dead or Santana snapped and they needed a soundtrack of words to pass the time. I quickly learnt that words, when they worked, could be as distinctive as a fancy guitar riff, and that I liked what I could do with a sentence in free flow. Suddenly I found that writing could be as much fun as reading. Or even more fun. That was all there was to it. I wanted to write for the fun of it. For myself and for anyone who happened to read what I wrote. To put into words what I was feeling, and what I could see, and to play with the words until it felt like life. I didn't think of making a book, or going any further. Tickling one reader, or two, was enough. Publishing and all that goes with it belonged to another world. To write was to play, and that was all that mattered.

The advice

At that vulnerable age, when every adult wants to know what you want to be when you grow up and you can't tell the truth, which is that all you want is to grow up, nothing more, I let slip that I wanted to be a writer. I didn't mention fiction or poetry and hoped there was some other kind of writing in which I could disguise myself and my pleasures. My father's friends, newspaper men with glasses of Scotch in their fists, laughed their heads off. This was Manila in 1970. We were living in a surreal world. If you were a journalist stuck there with Marcos running the show, all you could do was laugh your head off.

One said, 'You'd better go to London, then. On Fleet Street you'll learn what writing really is.'

The other said, 'Manchester. Go work for *The Guardian*. Start with the printers. Your thumbs have to turn black with ink. You need to know how words are made, even if you can't spell.'

These guys were writers, and even though not the kind I wanted to be, they were closer to it than anyone else I knew. I understood what they meant. My fingers were already blackened, and reddened, from fiddling with two-tone typewriter ribbons, threading them from spool to spool, and cleaning the inverted letters on the typebars. I used my fingers already. My thumbs were the only bits of my hands I didn't use to write. I tried to use all my other fingers on the keys, and the heel of my palm for the scroll lever to crank the paper and shoot the carriage back. Only now, 40-plus years later, have I got around to using my thumbs to touch the screen of this or that tablet, or a smartphone, to jot the fragments of the next novel on.

But they were right to tell me to learn how to make words with my hands. Although boozy and loquacious, they knew the secret was to use your hands rather than your mouth. And that is what all that Beat typing and spontaneous writing taught me. To love the pleasure of words flowing from your fingers: the tactile sensuality of words. For me that is not restricted to paper, ink and manual typewriter keys. Hammering keys is a special pleasure, but so is the light touch that detonates the letters of an electric typewriter – my mammoth Olivetti that I got in my twenties, which used to shake the house with the recoil of the carriage return, allowing me to kid myself about the power of words – or the silky ripples of the newly invented computer screen, as you stroked a keyboard to conjure up a sentence. The difficulty is to play with words, have fun with them, and still get them in the right order.

Starting to write

In the early 1980s, after a decade of writing poems, moving from the random to the precise, from Ginsberg to Lowell, after the relief of abandoning my magic realist novel – thanks to *Midnight's Children* there was no need to go down the Márquez road of solitude anymore – I started to spend more time on stories. The physicality of writing still ruled everything. The flow of words constantly checked by the frustration of lining carbon paper or changing ribbons. And then learning the economics of rewriting, trying to keep edits to as few pages as possible so that you don't need to retype the lot. Cutting and pasting bits of paragraphs, sentences, even words, to reduce the cost of photocopying – 5p per page – at the corner shop. William Burroughs and Brion Gysin had nothing on my scissors-and-tape technique. In my own way, I followed the advice I was given. I learnt to use my fingers to make sentences. I began to think that writing that did more than record the moment was worth trying to do. I thought perhaps to get a poem or a story published would be something worthwhile. The lessons came then. Cryptic lessons in the form of tersely worded rejections from heartless magazine editors: 'Not for us,' 'Not good enough,' 'Try again', 'Almost liked this'. That was what feedback was in the 1970s and 1980s. A virtual writing workshop not so much in cyberspace as in self-addressed brown manila envelopes and second class stamps that took months to get from one letter box to another. It was the best I could have had at the time, but it was slow. Years would go by on one poem. I learnt to be patient. I would spend weeks trying to work out why some anonymous reader at some magazine would respond so differently from those friends I had so easily entertained in my adolescence. I realized then that spontaneous writing is fine for yourself and your immediate circle, but to reach beyond it and to retain immediacy beyond the immediate moment, you need to rewrite. You need to rewrite until the story, the poem, becomes a thing itself.

The breakthrough came when *Stand Magazine* took my story 'The Storm Petrel'. The first draft was written before the violence that led to a 30-year war broke out in Sri Lanka in July 1983. The title came in the later drafts when I saw that the real world and my imagined one shared the same page. I learnt that it is something more than a metaphor that touches the heart.

That story also brought me my agent, then just starting out too, who asked if I had thought of sending a story to *Granta*. I hadn't. So, for the next year or two, I sent story after story to *Granta* until I had warm and encouraging letters from everyone who worked on the magazine except the editor − all of them appreciative and encouraging, but always ending with a firm and inevitable rejection. Nothing was ever good enough.

Then one day I sent them the longest story I had ever written. It might have been IBM's new monster-sized portable PC that my father-in-law handed down, with its five and a quarter inch floppy disk where you could cut and paste again and again, limitlessly, using only a keyboard, or Sinclair's crazy Z88 that I got my employers to buy for me, where you could carry your pipe dreams with you digitally on a tiny three-line screen − but something allowed me to keep going with a story, so that it broke the 4,000-word barrier that I had always stalled at before. And this one, for the first time, was set entirely in the country of my birth, Sri Lanka.

I got a call to come and meet the boss. The Granta office in those days was over a hairdresser's on the outskirts of Cambridge. A busy bearded man popped out of a room and beamed. He sat me down and asked some random questions which I dodged as best I could. Then he told me he would like to publish my story. I wondered why he couldn't just put that on a comp slip just like any other magazine editor. Something positive in writing to weigh against the stack of polite rejections I had built up over the years.

'But we have to publish your first book as well. And the next,' he added. *Granta* had just started a new book-publishing venture.

After years of trying to get a new story published, I suddenly found a publisher demanding a book. I thought it couldn't get better than that.

When I did deliver my first book, a collection of nine stories, he seemed surprised. He said he was expecting a novel. I suspect he then began to doubt whether a novel would ever come from such slim beginnings, especially given the sort of novels being written at the time.

The plan

My plan for the novel was to write an abstract, metaphysical prose poem set in a white room with no specific location. I wanted the place to be as far from the locations of my book of stories as it could be. I had done enough, I thought, to stretch my map of the imagined world with *Monkfish Moon*. This would be a novel of two voices, nothing more. A reef knot tying Becket to Nabokov. I failed from page one. The room quickly took root in Colombo. A garden grew fast around it. The walls dampened in the humidity. Ranjan Salgado, at the centre of the novel, began to sweat.

I began to see different possibilities. A novel like the ones I started to read when I had moved on from pulp fiction and Dharma Bums to Greene, Naipaul, Fitzgerald, to books that immersed you in an imagined world within about 180 pages. The kind of book you could carry in your pocket, and which opened a world you could carry in your head.

My first attempt at a novel, in the late 1970s, had floundered in too many abstract ideas, the seductive promises of magic realism and grand plans. This time I kept to the simplest of plans. I had learnt from writing short stories to keep my plans small. They had to fit on a compliments slip – from that pile of rejections – and be easy to understand at a glance. A line here and a line there. My first note about the novel is on an even smaller piece of paper. A page from the jotting pad you get next to the phone in a hotel room. Jianguo Hotel, Beijing, in this case. I was at the Jianguo in March 1992. I only know that because I wrote it down. I was there on a tour I was doing for my job that took me everywhere but the location of my story. In my box of old papers and typescripts for this first novel, there are similar scraps of paper from the Regent in Taipei and the Seoul Plaza Hotel. But on the back of the Beijing notepaper is the main plan: a time-line to work out the relative ages of the narrator Triton and the central character Ranjan Salgado. And a little wave-like line that was meant to indicate the arc of the story. A similar piece of paper from a year later gives two new alternative titles: *Reef* or *Wave*.

But the most elaborate plan I can now find in the box is not about the story or the shape of the novel, but a timetable for writing the book. Two sheets of Filofax-sized paper show how I hoped to balance the needs of a new job, home life, young kids and writing month by month. I had got serious about the vague hopes of writing that I had day-dreamed about for years. My appointments diary for the year shows that I'd negotiated to use my leave (paid and unpaid) mostly as a day off every couple of weeks for writing. And there is a 3 × 5 index card with a weekly routine that states: 6:00–7:30 a.m. every morning on the novel, before going to work, with an extra 8 hours spread around every weekend. With that beside my computer (by 1992 I had progressed to a chunky portable Panasonic computer with a greyscale screen a third of the size of a page of A4), I wrote the book that I thought was the story of Mister Salgado and Miss Nili. All I wanted at first was to show Mister Salgado's world through the eyes of Triton, the narrator. Everything had to be coloured through what he knew, what he believed, what he felt. His politics, his history, his language, his longing. If one wanted authenticity, there was no room for tricks. I took to heart Raymond Carver's exhortation – 'no gimmicks' – and tried to write the book Triton would write, never thinking anyone would notice him as anything but the teller of the tale. I expected him to be one of those ciphers I had grown up with – an invisible voice. I knew he had to grow, but I didn't expect him to take centre stage. That was a surprise. The book turned out to be full of surprises for me.

It was in the second dive into the novel, when I set about rewriting it, that I began to see a different story from the one I had started with. The book I had written was not quite the same as the one I had thought I was writing. It had started as a 'Whisper' – that was the original working title. I was looking for a voice. And then I noticed the reef that the central character Mister Salgado was obsessed with, and began to see a line that combined even as it divided, like a pencil line that an artist might draw to create a shape within and without. My eye had been on Mister Salgado and the woman who walks into his life, Miss Nili. Their affair was meant to be the main story but then, slowly, the eye of the narrator became the focus, and then his voice. I began to see that the book was becoming the story of Triton. It was a surprise. I was glad. You need to be surprised by what you write. A book needs something more than the words you pour into it. But getting the words right is the first step.

A year after I started, I had a draft ready to send to my champion (the deputy editor) at *Granta*. His response was a three-page letter that pointed out all the flaws still in the novel, in terms of structure and detail, but with a hint that if I could address them, then it might just work and become something special. It was the best advice. After that, several other editors played pass the parcel. One reminded me of grammar and the past pluperfect, another helpfully pointed out the overwritten paragraphs, another pencilled in 'ugh' to what I had thought was my best line. All were helpful, but the main shift came from that first editorial letter. I took the whole thing more seriously because he did.

My plans and notes expanded from a leaf from a jotting pad into a single A4 sheet of paper. But it was still essentially a time-line to make sure I knew what was happening in the story and outside the story in the period of the novel. It was for this next draft that I started on serious research. Regular visits to the newspaper library in Colindale, where I read every Sri Lankan newspaper of the period to check that what was being sold, what was being talked about, each month of the story was accurate. I wrote to aquatic agencies and Greenpeace to find out who knew what about the state of coral reefs. I don't think I had any replies, but I became a bit like my marine biologist Mister Salgado in the book, and read everything available on the subject. I did whatever was required to find out what I needed. In the final stages, I went out to a coral reef to check out the fish, as I was lucky enough to be travelling near one. I asked my mother in Sri Lanka to ask her cook what he knew about a legendary story I wanted Triton to recount. I questioned teachers of English as a foreign language to find out how fast Triton could master English. I wanted the details to work at every level, although I had no idea what the overall effect might turn out to be. Now, looking back I can see how little I knew about what I was doing as I wrote and rewrote. I printed out each version in a different font, or layout, as though I needed to see the story survive whatever physical form it was put into. Remembering that early advice from the Manila newspapermen, I tried to physically handle the words, and the paper, in every way I could. I wanted to know what this novel was, in its essence, but it still eluded me. It still surprises me.

Autobiography

The source of your fiction is yourself, but that does not mean a first novel has to be autobiographical. One does have to write oneself out before fiction can flower, but this can be in stories, poems and all the other writing one does. Someone suggested that if you wrote 100,000 words about yourself and discarded them, then you might be ready to write fiction. I counted all those rejected stories over the years and reckoned I had just about got there. When it came to writing this novel, I was ready to write about everything but me. I wanted the story to seem like an autobiography, but not mine. I set my novel in 1970 Colombo, which was exactly when I wasn't there, but the story allowed me to bring in things I had seen elsewhere and at other times and transform them into what was needed by the book.

So, Triton as a cook made dishes I had known, but in ways new to me. Miss Nili uses a makeshift sauna I remember seeing in my childhood, but with a heat I didn't know was possible. The merchants on the road, the act of revenge with a chili powder in our neighbourhood, wandered in into my mind, so I put them in. Triton the narrator I cooked up with bits from all the many cooks I have known. In all of these what was important was some feeling behind the words and images that made my heart race. The autobiography of real value in fiction is the emotions of the writer at the point of writing. At the end of his forensic *Lectures on Literature*, Vladimir Nabokov says, 'I have tried to teach you to read books for the sake of their form, their visions, their art. I have tried to teach you to feel the shiver of artistic satisfaction, to share not the emotions of the people in the book but the emotions of its author – the joys and difficulties of creation'. The focus makes sense to me. Even if you don't put yourself in the book, you become the book.

'Every author in some way portrays himself in his works, even if it be against his will.' – Johann Wolfgang von Goethe.

Against his will is important.

But occasionally something that happens off the page is too good to lose and fits in the frame unaltered. There is a red Volkswagen in my first novel, which is similar to the one I used to drive. I sold it a week after the book went to press. The last time I had filled the tank, I'd driven into a petrol station in North London manned by a young man from Sri Lanka who called me in to help him work the till. . . . That incident solved the problem of how I should begin the novel. I didn't need to make much up. I wrote it pretty much as it happened – the way I used to write in the heady days when I first started and wanted to write down what happened as it happened. But it came at the end, after I had imagined the rest of the novel.

My lessons

Looking back, I can now see that I should have learnt a great deal from writing my first novel. I should have, but I didn't. I should have learnt not to doubt that I would finish the book I eventually embark on. I shouldn't doubt it, but I always do. I should have learnt not to let anything distract me from the next sentence, but I am constantly distracted and lose my way every day. I should have learnt that the novel has to become the most important thing and that it will draw everything around me into it and become, at least for a moment, the whole world. That I do recognize, but I still try to keep it at bay. I do know that a novel needs time; you have to give it time. Lots of time. It is the best thing you could do with time. But I have not yet learnt how to do that. I always have to discover it anew. I am waylaid by doubt, tripped up by distractions and I forget what I am doing and lose time by the bucketful. But then, every now and again, a miracle happens, and one word follows another and another. You settle down for the long haul expecting the next book to take 6 years like the last and discover a first draft has appeared before you knew what you were doing. Then you realize you can never tell what will happen when it comes to writing fiction. It is always a surprise.

Elements

Beginnings and preparation

A. L. Kennedy

We'll begin with your novel's beginning. To be as simple as possible – it has to convince the reader to stay with it. The reader has other things to do – your novel must supersede those things. How it does this will, naturally, vary widely. The writer will deploy mechanisms involving drama, threat, mystery, empathy, lyricism. . . . The list is a long one. What will make those mechanisms work will be a sense that this opening, this first paragraph, this first sentence, absolutely knows where it's going and it is full of the flavour and touch and life of how it will proceed and whom it will reveal. It has confidence. Before the reader can believe, it has belief. It summons and the reader must follow.

How do we achieve belief and certainty? By believing and being certain. That is to say, we cultivate contagious belief by understanding the nature of the story we have to tell and knowing the characters we will portray. Simple, but not easy. But simple.

If you read the first paragraph of any working novel you will find the same thing – utter assurance, a setting out of tones, hints, colours, tastes, shadows and promises, just as they should be. Here is only a little of the whole animal, but we know it really is an animal and we know we will meet it all in the end.

What follows will deal with how we arrive at the kind of certainty that will make a total stranger suspend their usual activities and spend their time with our lies.

Who are you?

The last thing many writers (and particularly novelists) need to be is even a little more self-regarding. Nevertheless, I do think it's appropriate and useful to take personal stock before we begin a large piece of work. Our novel will be with us for a long time, so it would be sensible to inventory our available strengths and weaknesses before we begin. Some of these will speak directly to elements we know are going to be part of the specific work, and some will begin, or continue, our process of knowing who we are as writers so that we can improve.

Useful questions to ask might be: What genuinely interests me at the moment? Does this novel reflect my concerns? Will it contain enough of my passions – private, political, musical, sporting, whatever – to be sustainable for me and rewarding for the reader? Is my prose ready for this? If I look at earlier work, is there a good match between my sentence structure and my ability to punctuate and control meaning? Is there a good strong match between the part of my voice I want to give my reader and my current style? (And when I say part of my voice, I am aware that the novel will eat almost all your available colours of voice at one time or another.) Am I funny? Am I moving? Am I serious? Am I scary? In what proportions? Will those proportions help me to tell this novel's story and to present this novel's characters, in as far as I am aware of them currently? Are these central characters going to be bearable to have around for as long as they'll need to be? How do I respond to people? What kind of stories do I like telling them? Is there something I am hiding from in this piece of work, any issue I am avoiding? (The issues we flee – and novels always throw them up – are often very fertile if we simply explore them.) Am I easily distracted, or an over-worker? Do I need silence to work, or music? Am I great under the gun, or slow and steady? How am I with stress? Will showing my partner my work be a good thing? Will my partner really wanting to see my work be a good thing? Will their not being bothered about my work at all be a good thing? When am I most productive and can I arrange to work then? Do I truly feel prepared enough to begin?

Who is your reader?

In some cases this is a question with a very specific and sometimes time-limited answer. If your reply is, 'Teenagers who long for vampires.' Or 'Middle-aged mums who would like to read e-porn.' Then you may have missed the boat. If your reader is intended to be a 10–14 year old, or a military history buff, or a lover of romance, Sci-Fi or any of the other available genres as purveyed by a particular imprint . . . then you need to be sure that you please both the publisher's idea of their market and the actual market.

There is also a rather deeper question which speaks to the relationship you wish to establish with your reader as an individual. This transcends genre. I believe that the finest crime fiction, children's stories, literary fiction – the finest writing, full stop, always addresses the reader with deep care and attention. This care and attention is the fruit of compassion, respect, generosity and a type of love, the necessary amount of love, to allow the reader to feel you are talking to them and only them. Writers are often narcissistic – at this level, readers are always narcissistic. Why shouldn't they be? You have climbed into their head, of course they want you to be talking to them and only them – otherwise you're some kind of witlessly mouthy burglar. If this sounds nauseatingly impractical or indulgent, think of it another way. The more your reader believes you, the better your novel will prosper. The best way to get someone to believe you, especially when you're lying – and a novel is one great, big lie – is to be sincere. So you need to work out your particular way of successfully faking sincerity. Practically speaking, one of the easiest and least tiring ways is by being sincere. You don't have to fake knowing what you're talking about if you actually do.

Environment

You may not be able to control all of the environmental factors that ease or disrupt your writing process, but it is often possible to do more than you'd think to give yourself an easy life. Novels take long-term concentration. If you need non-intrusive company, maybe you should sit in a coffee shop. If you need isolation, can you blag a residency somewhere? Can you claim a room of your own, ring-fence an area of a room, or a timeslot in a room, slap on some headphones and make your family, or surroundings go away for a while, at least in auditory terms? It may be that you need to negotiate with the people around you that when you're apparently staring into space, it doesn't mean you can be talked to; what's a fair way to signal you're 'busy' and what's a fair way to reward others for giving you space and – in some instances – effectively allowing an imaginary Other into their marriage.

Physical comfort is important – the right light, the right chair, the right keyboard – so take a bit of time experimenting to get your set-up fit for purpose, or re-testing what you already have. Heating bills are now an issue – is there a way you can keep warm without racking up kilowatt hours? You may turn off your phone, you may wish to cut off the Wi-Fi, too, or to install software that makes you enter a wearisomely long key before you can surf. And surfing can feel as if you're working – it uses your computer, you are still hitting keys. . . . Hours can be wasted in this way. There is software out there – Google Chrome provides a nanny function, among others – to help you to use your computer to limit your time between breaks and to limit your procrastination. The cheapest way to do both would be to use an alarm clock to govern your hours and to switch off your Wi-Fi, etc. other than at set times.

Your internal environment is also, of course, important. If you know what kind of person you are, you'll know if you need encouragement from others, bursts of physical activity, planned breaks to stop overworking, or a strict timetable to prevent you from slacking. It's very likely that your own worries and those of the world will intrude to some degree. But part of being an effective writer – especially on long work – involves creating a place of safety within which you proceed in a disciplined manner, as if all were well. If that means you meditate, practice Tai Chi, or talk to the walls, then do so. In the end, your writing will not only prosper if you offer it a place of safety – it can become one, particularly on a long project.

Health

Do remember to self-maintain. Long shifts may be exhilarating, but they're debilitating if they're a permanent feature. Being physically healthy will improve your mental stamina, and taking whatever exercise suits you can be incorporated into your thinking time. If your regime involves chain-smoking crack and a bottle of absinthe a day, best of luck to you – but it's easier to be a writer by writing than by being a cliché. If you're just not healthy in a long-term way and there's nothing to be done about it then writing is, of course, a way of being out of your body. If that's the case, do be aware that physical pain – like any other regular feature – will bleed into the work, and you want to control that, rather than letting it control you.

Routine

Different people react differently to the demands of long projects, but somehow we all have to get finished pages out there. We have to produce and planning a routine will help that. If we know who we are, we can play to our strengths. I hate having set hours, loathe early rising and will work like a donkey until I drop. So I write when it's dark, I vary my lengths of shift, try to incorporate treats and fix immoveable breaks. Setting aside time to be inspired by this or that is very useful in the long term − novels are draining. You don't have to be elevated about it. If strolling past the great masters doesn't do it for you, then you might just nip through to the living room and kiss someone, play some R&B, or have a bath. The novel, if you commit to it, will teach you about the things you really need to get you through it. In the process, it will teach you about creating something that will be there to get other people through other things. The novel's rigours are generous.

Nothing needs to be set in stone and if you live with other people, or animals, you're going to have to negotiate whose agenda wins and when. If you're any kind of carer you will have to divide yourself between the demands that press upon you in as sane a way as possible.

It's different for girls

Sorry, but it just is. If you're in a relationship, or have kids, or both, and if you're a writer and female your writing may well have a tendency to be less important than the 'Woman Stuff' that you're meant to be dealing with. I am about to generalize and I am often wrong and − in specific cases − can be very wrong, but *in general,* even today, male writers get on with the pages while things are taken care of. Female writers take care of things and have to fit pages in around doing so. I say that, fully aware that my male partner is entirely supportive of what I do and happy however I wish to do it. But then again he's as self-contained as it gets and creative himself, but in another area. Two writers in the same house. . . . Well, I wouldn't try it.

But we can all − whatever our gender − try to act like writers who believe in what we do and who respect it and who will behave respectably in advance. We can hope others will do likewise. We may be in a position to ask them if they could. We may be unsuccessful and have to work around obstacles – that can fuel the energy of a book, if you let it – that can make you realize how precious your voice is to you and that it deserves your best efforts to perfect it. Building a place of safety, or finding a literal place of safety is not a minor issue here and can be soul-saving, if not life-saving. If you're with someone who reacts badly to your voice being audible at all, then they may react badly to your writing. Try and defend yourself and your work, or seek out others who can – a women's library, a library, a friend's house, a spot on a park bench – spaces that will welcome you.

Character and plot

While you've been looking at yourself and your surroundings you will also have been looking at your characters and their surroundings. The simplest way to put this would be – when you close your eyes and think of it, does the world of your book feel as real as the real world when you call it to mind? Do your principle characters feel as real as genuine human beings who happen not to be present? Are your smaller characters like real people, briefly glimpsed, but in necessary detail? If not, then why not?

There are probably as many ways of coming to this level of assurance as there are writers. If you know who you are, you'll know at least some ways to approach your investigations of character. Find out if it's what labels they wear that gets you in there, or what movies they love, their shoes – whatever works – you can play with this, explore. Generally, the more you look, the more you will find. Your mind will create something to be there when you look, in the same way it will make you hallucinate when you stare at blank white for too long.

If you know some events that happen in your novel, are they falling in a useful order? Would they logically generate other events? Have you picked the right tense to suit them? Is your point of view the best suited to your characters and the way they interact with the plot? Eventually the interplay of these elements can become organic, complex, satisfying, thrilling, whatever you want. But you have to know what you want and you have to supply yourself with enough material to work on. This is particularly important when you have interrupted time – planning and pondering can occupy you when you have to pick the kids up, or iron, or walk the dog, or take your lunch break from earning the money that will see you through until you get an advance.

If you don't plan enough before you begin to write, you will massively decrease your chances of finishing your novel successfully. From the moment you start writing your characters down, they will be visible. So they need to be visibly credible in your given situation. Your reader will learn about them as the story progresses – you have to have them present and real from the outset to a quite high degree in order for them to be effective as someone that can be learnt, who can live and speak and do what is necessary.

Busking your way into the story will mean you write without an awareness of plot progression and tone and a sense of the colour that should underpin your prose at any given time. Which is to say, you will be practicing writing less well than you should. Why would you want to do that when writing well is very hard and you only have one lifetime in which to become good at it?

Plan. Don't kill the thing's spontaneity, just know it sufficiently well so that you can tell it to someone else. That's what we do – we tell stories we know to other people so they can enjoy them. So know the story. Enough. If you know yourself, you'll have a fair idea of how much enough happens to be at the moment. Don't assume that your plan won't change – or panic if it does – but do have a good grip on your basics and a very good grip on your people. If your invented people can be psychologically and physically consistent within settings which are also doing their job, then the plot will be progressed as you'd hope and changes will be improvements, rather than collapses into despair.

Deep idea

This is another way of saying 'What is your novel about?' Even, 'Who is your novel?' Beyond the plot incidents and the nature of your characters, there will be central issues, themes, tropes, obsessions, concerns – you can use whichever terms please you. Deep in the heart of the huge creature which is a fully-formed novel there is something golden, something distilled, something which shapes and influences all other elements and which springs from all other elements. If you look at the overview of your elements you will find they tend to point towards these core ideas – without this level of consideration you may well have trouble really making your novel complete. Alphabets of imagery, successful titles and coherent themes all tend to spring from this core – whether you're writing for pre-teens, or guys who like guns, or book groups in Middle England.

Support networks

You're about to do something difficult for a long period of time – try to set in place things that will support you. You will be looking after your health, but others may join you in this – a massage now and then for tired shoulders could help, or a timely visit to a healthcare professional if you're actually ill. If you have an editor or agent (or both) waiting for your novel then you're remarkably fortunate and you can use them to bounce ideas around. Try and set up how that will work, how much time they can give you and which problems they're going to be able to help with. (Remember that people may not be right about how helpful they are in in this or that area.) If you are going to need resources, have them at hand or accessible before you set out, in as far as you can. That can apply to reference books, or fresh cups of tea. You can lose your thread quite easily if you have to keep making trips to see such and such a location, or trawl the internet. Or boil a kettle. Make life easy for yourself. If you're a group person, maybe you need the help of a writer's group – who'll want you to help back – or just to hang out with friends for a rest. Maybe you have one mind you chime well with – perhaps discuss how that will work if you call on his or her reading time. If your domestic situation is gruelling, make sure you know that it doesn't define you as someone who deserves discomfort, and seek out people and forums within which you get some nourishment, whether that's mental, physical, spiritual, online, in person, on the phone, or variations on all those. And – of course – if you have prepared your characters well enough and know them, they will be waiting to set out with you. They will be eager. They will wake you in the morning, ready to press on. As the novel progresses, they will support you more and more.

Setting, place and atmosphere

Romesh Gunesekera

Elmore Leonard, a sharp writer, acclaimed for his dialogue and pace, has no time for the elements that might make up atmosphere. The weather, for example. In his famous ten rules for writing, the first is: never begin with the weather. Fair enough, you might say. Long before Elmore Leonard you can find wonderful and varied writers for whom the weather is inconsequential and who do not start with anything like it to establish atmosphere. Jane Austen, for example, whose opening sentence in *Pride and Prejudice* is probably the best known:

> 'It is a truth universally acknowledged, that a single man in possession of a good fortune must be in want of a wife.'

The whole novel is there. (But we still want all the rest. It is worth working out why.)

Or Melville's 'Call me Ishmael', which opens *Moby Dick*. Melville is interesting in this context. He is one who does handle weather and for whom atmosphere is important. As indeed it is for Emily Brontë. Imagine *Wuthering Heights* without the harsh bleak atmosphere that permeates the book. Or take the opening of Arundhati Roy's much loved *The God of Small Things*:

> 'May in Ayemenem is a hot, brooding month. The days are long and humid. The river shrinks and black crows gorge on bright mangoes in still, dustgreen trees. Red bananas ripen. Jackfruits burst. Dissolute bluebottles hum vacuously in the fruity air. Then they stun themselves against clear windowpanes and die, fatly baffled in the sun.'

Perhaps we need to think a little more about what we mean by atmosphere, place and setting.

Readers do want to know where a story is set. They want a sense of the place and they look for the atmosphere conjured up by the words. But they can find this from the slimmest of information.

Writers know that some of these elements are changeable. It is hard to imagine Huckleberry Finn floating down the Nile instead of the Mississippi, or Mr Biswas building his house in Birmingham, but perhaps that is because we haven't tried. Movie makers and theatre directors have shown us how a story can be shifted quite radically in time and place and still be the same story: Macbeth does not have to be set in Scotland, Dostoevsky can be relocated in today's world in Florida or Azerbaijan, even Mr Darcy can survive Bollywood. It is of course easier with plays where the setting is often noted only in a line or two and there is usually plenty of room to manoeuvre. But when it comes to a novel where the setting, the place and the atmosphere have been painstakingly evoked, such a change means that you have a different book. That suggests a novel is something more than the story it contains. And this we know the moment we begin to write one.

Although everything in a novel can change, and often does change as one rewrites it, once you reach the final version every element in it has to seem exactly right. Within drafts, you can decide that the Nile delta is the better location, or indeed the outer rings of Birmingham, but at some point it has to become the one and only possible place. Yeats, speaking of poetry, said: 'Our words must seem to be inevitable'. I think that applies to novels too.

The question for the novelist on page one, or even before he or she gets there is: how much do I decide before I start and how much do I need to know?

Hemingway says: 'Try to write on the principle of the iceberg. There is seven-eighths under water for every part that shows.'

To begin with, I think, it doesn't really matter how much you know beforehand. If it is too little, you'll find out more; if it is too much you will have to forget some of it. I don't know what the great novelists we admire might have known about their novels before they started. I imagine Moby Dick didn't just breach the page unexpectedly. I doubt Madame Bovary started out as Nefertiti bored in Egypt. But I suspect that these characters and the nature of the places they are rooted in, even if it is the ocean, evolved as the book grew. That evolution may be very swift, and happen hour by hour, paragraph by paragraph, or it may take years, and draft after draft.

To start you don't need anything but the urge to write. But if you do have the bones of a story, a glimmer of a setting, it does help to get started. First time novelists seem to either have a very firm and clear idea of the book they want to write (based on an experience, their life or an obsession), or they have no idea at all of what they want to write, but they do have an irresistible urge to write a novel. In both cases the writing of a novel is a way of discovering what you *can* write as opposed to what you *want* to write. All sorts of things come into play that will determine this, from the configuration of your brain, your archive of memories, your physical state, your health and whatever else is going on in your life. It is no different from any other physical and mental activity: whether it is a high jump or a crossword puzzle. Writing a novel is laborious. It has surprisingly tough physical and mental demands, given that it seems all you need to do is sit down and pick up a pencil or jab a keyboard. You will find some things within reach and that some are not for you, however much you may train for them.

So what should a writer do? How can one start?

1. Understand that the novel is the king. Whatever goes in it must work for it. If it needs Cyprus, Palermo or a skyway to Saturn, it must have it.

2. Remember, all details are changeable, from the temperature of the room to the colour of the flowers in the geranium pot. So pick what works for now.

3. Choose a location. The time and the place. Although you might like to locate your story in some ambiguous place, at some point it has to become a specific place: the location of your story. Your reader needs to know that they are somewhere, even if it is never-never land.

4. Remember the real place of a novel is in the imagination.

5. The atmosphere of a novel can be the atmosphere of a place, or the mood of the story. Your reader wants to feel it, otherwise they will close the book. So make sure they feel it.

6. Decide the importance of the place and the atmosphere. If it has no effect on the characters or what happens in the story, then don't waste time on it. But if it is something that affects the way in which the characters behave and think, then work on it and show it. Readers do want to go places, both familiar and unfamiliar. But you have to take them there.

7. Think hard about what you need to tell and what you need to show. A good way to remember this is to inscribe Chekhov's famous phrase on your laptop or your heart:

> 'Don't tell me the moon is shining; show me the glint of light on broken glass.'

8. Write. Write more. Write some more. The material you need will be in the words you put down.

Characters

A. L. Kennedy

Work involving a character is both wonderful and utterly frustrating. A believable character can make a reader forgive all manner of sins. A wooden cast member can wreck a fine plot. On the one hand we are hugely lucky to be writing for other human beings who generally share our range of senses and our range of emotions. So we can use our own reactions to our writing as a kind of guide to theirs. And we will generally only be portraying human beings to the reader – that, or other relatively human-like beings. This should help us. And yet we have to be aware that failures to make our characters successfully real within their given context will be the easiest flaws for the reader to spot. Human beings are hugely alert to images which resemble their own faces – finding them on Mars, in grilled cheese sandwiches, window smears. They notice even subtly unusual features – for example, when a face is overly symmetrical. Every day we recognize, love, judge, trust, obey and simply know each other by processing layers of complex information, all of it about being human and with humans. Readers are used to the real world offering them real people and getting things right in detail, so we have to be painstaking in our portrayal of fictional people.

Moral and personal issues

Every writer, I would hope, has people in his or her life. We all have the opportunity to decide whether we will protect those close to us when we create characters. Making no active decision will still produce some kind of position on the privacy of others and it is probably best to address this in a way that ensures long-term comfort. You can decide whether you make use of people you know and render them in print in a manner that leaves them recognizable and therefore perhaps uncomfortably revealed. You can decide whether you make public, for example, family history. You can decide whether the end of a relationship demands a novel of revenge, or whether your book will be mainly an attempt at immortalizing yourself as a protagonist. Some of these decisions will clearly impact on your personal life. A loving and generous impulse might mean we wish to celebrate our loves by portraying them, or reflecting them, but may cause others to feel exposed. Writing for a loved one can be hugely energizing, but in this context it can mean that the author becomes overly-constricted by what they know of reality and can't shape material dispassionately in a way that serves the narrative and the reader. A novel may partly become a closed conversation with one, unseen reader – that can be a problem.

So I would suggest that creating a fiction out of non-fictional material has pitfalls. Your fiction may take real elements and inspirations as starting points, but these will always have to serve the demands of the novel. Speaking practically, rather than morally, it can be easier to just make things up.

The chicken and the egg

So how do we make our characters? In outlining any given inspiration a writer may be accurately modelling their process, but I think very often they will be simplifying a very dynamic process. We have a fragment of plot, and it may make a female character inevitable. (Let's say, giving birth.) We may then concentrate on this fragment of information to examine what this female would do in that situation. (Be brave, be drugged, die, be helped by her lover, betray her lover to her husband?) The answer to these exploratory questions will suggest more details about our woman. (She's of an age to give birth – that's still a wide age range. . . . A 48-year old with a lover? A young corpse whose husband will travel the novel scarred by grief and worried by childcare costs. . . ?) There is a constant interplay between elements.

We also have to factor in, as we work, whether what we know of our characters may influence what tense we use. If our pregnant woman is the main protagonist and dies . . . is it sensible to tell the whole story in flashback?

What are the limitations of that? Do we want to raise the stakes as she plans and hopes, do we risk making it all boring because she's going to die? Do we dodge right in the final chapter and save her? Is that a cheap manoeuvre? If our heart is set on it, how do we justify it?

Our characters are also worked upon by those around them, or generate gaps which we must fill with people who will fit them and fit their companions. Beyond this, always, the motor of the plot is running, as are its themes. If the novel is about guilt and we are sure of that – her death becomes charged in that direction. If the novel is about joy, or death, or children . . . our approaches will change. During the planning stages we can ask many questions, reform many strategies, break down and reassemble many critical masses of material. This can seem bewildering, or scary, but it allows us to know where we're going and to create people who seem to belong in the world they inhabit.

The consideration of point of view is, of course, deeply linked to character and to our principle characters. We have to consider carefully – and perhaps repeatedly – what voice or voices will suit our narrative and its characters. If the intimacy and immediacy of first person is a good choice, can we make use of that lack of overview, will we maintain clarity, given what we know of our character's psychology? Does our character discover things in real time as we do? Would first person aid this? Or perhaps the balance of flexibility, insight and perspective that comes from close third is what we need. Or are we handling many characters, quite a few of them important, are they travelling a good deal, experiencing much, passing through long periods of time? Would an omniscient third suit it best? This in turn interacts with plot and tense decisions. One set of solutions will tend to seem much more right than any other – if it doesn't, usually that's an indication that there's more work to be done.

Once we have a fair fix on voice, we can begin to see how a voice and a character bleed into each other and explore how a character's tone, vocabulary, passions, psychology and reactions to events give rise to a cascade of effects in the narrative and reflect back on our characters. We can aim to build a positive cycle. This can be explored before we write and enlarged upon when we do.

Different genres require different levels of character exploration, and this is another factor that will affect what you choose to put on the page and how.

A pacey spy thriller, or a piece of erotica might be light on passages of dense interior exploration. But a sense that events are happening to someone worth our attention and the ability to summarize character quickly and clearly come from in-depth knowledge. Offering key details helps our reader – so we have to find what the key details are.

Generation of elements

Different authors have different approaches here. I have known writers to model or draw characters in order to know them better. I have known others to pick out photographs or voices on which to base the beginnings of a person. I think that once we have had any kind of initial inspiration – *it's a woman, she's pregnant* – we can gain a good deal simply by examining the implications of what we already have. And at the planning stage these can always be abandoned, or new pathways can be followed when they seem more productive – *the male nurse who is unpleasant to her is more interesting.*

Be aware that characters you don't like need special attention – otherwise you will skimp on their details and they will seem unreal and therefore not function properly. You don't have to like everyone you write but, at a practical level, it is useful to love them and give them the level of attention necessary. You can at least love that they are so perfectly unlikeable. And show the details of that appropriately.

Borrowing techniques from drama can be very useful. Actors have been stared at while remembering lines, with only some sense of being someone else to defend them – they have developed various ways of finding character. You may wish to use the 'hot seating' technique, which involves others asking you questions in order to propel you into character as you answer for your person, using 'I'. You may wish to visit locations, study pastimes and adopt hobbies or habits that your characters seem to have or could explore. You can do something as simple as going for coffee once a week, while trying to see your street as they would.

Your hierarchy of sense will guide you into a more vivid appreciation of who they are and how they perceive the world – visual, olfactory, a blend of musical and tactile, non-visual, intensely olfactory . . . you decide what's best. You can use your own strongest senses as gateways to a totality of information for your character.

Simply asking questions of your character is deeply useful. If you ask the questions you'd expect from small talk at a party, you'll get bland answers and little material that has real life to it. If you ask about the core of their beings, they will tell you – you're their boss, their creator. This trains your mind to expect answers, and to think of your character as a separate entity with a real life. Even the frustrations of finding a way through your plot – *Why did you leave your wife?* – can become a help. Perhaps a major storyline involves your husband finding out why he left her, or never knowing why, or his being murdered by her because she can't think why he would have and has been troubled by the fact.

With robust characters, you can accompany your reader through your plot with success. Without them, you're not going to hold the interest of people who are used to people and the fascinations they provide.

Point of view and perspective

Romesh Gunesekera

The most important lesson I ever learnt about writing was the lesson about point of view (POV). These days anyone who has glanced at a writing manual, or dipped their toe in a writing circle, will have an inkling of POV. You can quickly become an expert at it and mention it in the way a chef might toss carpaccio into a conversation. But until about 1990 I didn't know much about it. I am sure I must have come across the term; for years I'd thumbed through all the writing books I could find, I'd wallowed in the water holes where quotes on writing from famous writers are gathered, I'd tried to find out how to write in every way – short of actually writing – for many years; but I didn't really appreciate what POV meant until I started rewriting the stories of my first book.

Until then POV meant only what it seemed to say: the POV from which a story is told. But it is a much more powerful tool than that. It is a way of seeing that alters everything. Now it feels like the only element of writing

I have some certainty about. When in doubt I look for the POV. But the moment I look closely I begin to get confused. Do I mean the issue of first person (the narrator is the 'I'), the second person (the use of 'you') or the third person (omniscient narrator who speaks of he, she, they . . .) Or does it mean the perspective, or viewpoint, of the main character, or any character? In practical terms, for you the writer trying to write your novel, it means both. It is whether you use 'I', 'you' or 'he/she', and the perspective from which the story is told.

Most of what I had read, or glanced at, about writing and how to do it, left me unsatisfied. Intuitively I knew that novel writing could not be separated into practice sessions and the real thing. There are no warm-up exercises for writing fiction. You can't practice writing a first novel in the third person. You can only do it for real, and if the piece of writing doesn't work, you either make it better or you do another. But each time you have to do it for real. The only writing book that made sense to me in those days was Dorothea Brande's *How to Become a Novelist*. It can still remind me of some useful ideas on temperament, on seeing, on the unconscious, but it does have gaps. It does not say much about POV.

In most writing books POV is mentioned, but most references to it make POV sound like one of a number of the different elements one needs to think about. But it is not the case that POV is simply one of the many elements of narrative. You can do without dialogue. You can do without description. You can do without place, or atmosphere or any of the other elements you normally find in narrative, and which we might discuss elsewhere in this book. But you cannot do without POV. Every story has a POV, and in every story it can change. It is the most important decision you have to make as a writer: which POV to use in the story. And the choice is yours. Luckily it is a decision you can reverse or change any number of times, until you find one that you will stick with.

There is no better way of understanding the power of POV than by working with it. Take a story you have written. Perhaps the best story you have written. What POV is it told from? Why? Is that the best POV to use? Are you sure? Change it and rewrite it and see if you still think so. Change the

POV of someone else's story (e.g. Edgar Alan Poe or Arthur Conan Doyle) and see what happens.

New writers like multiple points of view. There is a strange attraction that we have to writing from different points of view, as we have for using multiple voices. This is perhaps because we intuitively understand the idea that we no longer live in a world of one dominant narrative. But multiple points of view and multiple voices should not be used as a crutch. Don't do it because you can't handle the single voice or because boredom has set in. Use it only if it has to be used. Otherwise resist the urge, because if it is done simply because you think it looks daring and modern it will be neither of those, but merely an unnecessary display of technique.

My first experience of making conscious decisions on POV was in the stories I wrote for my first book. I remember one in particular: *Captives*. This is a story of a couple who arrive at a tourist hotel in Sri Lanka and explore a rock fortress. The original story was about the tensions in the relationship between the man and woman. My editor was more intrigued by the hotel manager who welcomed them, and asked me, 'What about him?' There was a spark in that hotel manager that seemed to have more life. So I retold the story from his POV. I changed it from third person to first person, but I also told it from his perspective. The whole story changed radically, from one about the couple to one about the man and his relationship to the couple. I discovered a more interesting story than the one I had intended to write.

My novels take much longer to write than they should, partly because I find I cannot decide on the best POV to use until I have written the novel. Only after I know the whole story am I able to work out how best to tell it. And that in turn changes the story. It is a long and laborious process and I haven't found a short cut. When I look at the boxes of typescripts around me as I go over and over a novel, I see that most of these scripts tell a different story. One that shifts with every shift in POV. I have one novel that started with three characters whose points of view were absurdly difficult: one was an amnesiac, the other could neither hear nor speak and the third was mad. I wanted three points of view, as the dialogue and interaction between them was hard to do, given their various difficulties in communication. Writing it was hard; reading it was harder. I changed my ideas on POV and put in a narrator who told the story. The three difficult characters mutated into characters with different sorts of difficulties. The novel, understandably, became a dystopian one, reflecting not only the world as I was seeing it then, but also the challenges of the writing.

Some writers learn faster. They are able to think through the story and then decide on the ideal POV in one go. If you are one of them, be thankful. You are lucky, and your novels will get written sooner than mine. But whatever kind of writer you are, do not neglect the power of the POV. It is not just another aspect of a novel: it is the vital element.

'An author in his book must be like God in the universe, present everywhere and visible nowhere.' – Gustave Flaubert

Voice, language and dialogue

A. L. Kennedy

Voice

Voice is, of course, at the heart of what we do as writers. As a long form, the novel will test narrative consistency, the ability to hold the reader over time, the ability to convey complex information and the ability to convey character in the manner required by our particular project. By consciously working to develop our voices, we can support our efforts in all these areas.

There is an intimate and very useful relationship between what I might call our own interior narrative – the voice in which we think – our customary verbal forms of address, and our voice on the page. Ideally, each should advance and encourage the other in a positive cycle. Certainly, if our writing on the page doesn't even resemble the way we would – most likely – address a stranger to whom we wish to give information in the best possible manner, appropriate to content, then we are likely to find ourselves producing stylistic errors and passages of obscure meaning, simply because we are working too far outside our comfort zones in terms of voice. We are familiar with the natural way that we express ourselves and are aware that stilted speech in ourselves or others is both unusual and a sign of some kind of tension. The same rules apply on the page, or rather in the musical space our words (should) open up in the reader's mind. The reader will be less likely to keep reading us if we convey tension, offer stilted phrases and a sense that all is not well.

One simple way to produce more natural prose would involve simply asking, 'How would I say this to someone? If I cut away the complication and anxiety and the weight of the novel leaning on my shoulders – how would I say this to someone?'

Although a great deal of emphasis in training courses, writing programmes and workshops is placed on literary elements and a kind of naming of parts, I feel that work with our speaking voices and an awareness and improvement of our ability to speak, to tell our stories, is extremely important. It can help to improve features of our writing automatically by dealing with the root causes of symptoms. If we are aware of our own voices and can feel them to be living, flexible and powerful things, this can feed directly into strong prose on the page.

So –

Explore voice exercises: there are many courses, tutors, books, DVD's and guides out there. Find someone you can work with who understands your specific needs as a writer and who can assist you. You might try joining a choir – this allows you to meet people you didn't invent earlier, improves breathing, health in general and your sense of yourself as a physical creature with a voice.

Any work in this area will improve your ability to read your own work in public, something many writers find gruelling. Reading to others should be a great opportunity to hear and see your voice affecting people, literally moving them. Rather than an occasion for nervousness, a good reading can give you a sense of power in your words – and if you've prepared yourself properly, are physically ready and have selected a reasonable section of prose (fairly self-contained, engaging), then you can promote your work, test your prose in progress and be reminded of the interaction at the core of your book – that between the story's 'teller' and the 'listener'.

Language and dialogue

The voice of our novel may well be coloured – particularly in first person, and close third person – by the voices of our characters. The language we use may not be standard to our narrative voice, it may be a mingling of our own style and that of one or more others. This is a great way to pass on information in depth without appearing to force exposition or to hold up the pace with plodding explanations. The choices we make will be based on our knowledge of our characters – and there is advice elsewhere on character work – but we may also want to look at how adept we are at passing on character knowledge through tone, or the absolutely transmitted voice of a character, either in direct speech or direct thought.

I can't emphasize enough that believable tone, dialogue, palettes of language and passages of thought all stem from thorough research on the individuals concerned.

Writers can get very panicked by dialogue and I am probably asked more questions about it than any other area. New writers tell me that they are 'not good at dialogue' far more frequently than they identify other weaknesses. This is, in part, because dialogue is the harshest test of character knowledge. You can use it as a diagnostic tool – if you truly can't get this or that character to speak as anyone in life ever would, then simply go back to your research and find more about the person in which you can believe.

You may also wish to use the old actor's trick of picking lines from different characters and trying to see if you can tell which person is speaking by looking at their sentence structure, tone and flavour. If everyone reads pretty much the same, then you're in trouble.

Beyond the panic, once you have a grip on who is speaking, the task may seem unfamiliar somehow, or more peculiar than simple prose, but it follows the same logic. Does this convey the information I need it to? Does this sound like something someone would ever say? If it doesn't, change it. Does this sound like something this person would ever say? If it doesn't, change it. Begin with how you might say it and work outwards, if that helps. Imagine saying the line down a telephone. With an awareness of how you best understand people, picture the person speaking, imagine the timbre of the voice speaking, think of the gestures accompanying and think of how the person feels, smells, tastes – whatever sense makes it real to you. Factor in whether you are showing things from their point of view or someone else's.

Writers also get very exercised about how to punctuate speech. The standard use of either single or double quotes, following the usual rules of the road, is familiar to the reader, and honestly isn't the ghastly interruption to you golden prose that you might suspect. Leaving out the punctuation gets very confusing unless you're fantastically good at rendering speech in a way that makes it instantly distinguishable from the surrounding prose. You could try putting a long dash before each speaker's lines, but do think twice before you leave it up to the reader to work out what's going on. This would also apply to thought. It may help, when thought leaks beyond highly coloured close third person to being rendered as a pseudo-interior monologue, if you italicize it, just for ease of understanding. And you might want to think about when you re-paragraph.

And give each speaker a new line – that also helps clarity. And it means you don't really even have to add *he said*. It's obvious that someone is speaking, and particularly if you're dealing with only two speakers, alternate lines will indicate them. This can give a real feeling of pace as you rock down the page. But remember that you're not writing for radio – if you give the reader undiluted dialogue for too long, you may actually lose a sense of character. Remember to give information about what's happening around the speakers, how they're moving, how they look – keep the whole scene alive. Some lines which are perfectly okay may become nonsensical if you don't give a sense of how they're said – *Yeah, right.* Is that sarcastic, apologetic, factual, grateful . . .? I don't know, yet.

Remember that if you describe a specific character and then segue into dialogue in the same sentence, or paragraph, there will be an assumption that the person you described is the one speaking. This makes life easy, because it cuts out some of the need to add she said or variations on that theme. Equally, it can be a disaster, if you have suddenly flipped to another character for the line.

I don't think anyone sane wants to write anything along the lines of 'He expostulated angrily'. That's too expositional, and I've probably never met anyone who has actually expostulated in my presence. (Perhaps I have been lucky.) Ideally, you leak in subtle information about the scene that makes on-the-nose statements of emotion superfluous. And your lines may do this anyway, they'll certainly help. If you write 'You crazy bitch from hell!', I may not need your helpful 'she shouted in annoyance'. He saids and she saids are inoffensive, but they can become tediously repetitive; and if you're using layout properly, some if not all of them will be superfluous.

If you are dealing with a scene that has multiple speakers, then simply be careful that we know who's saying what, and remember to vary the means by which you do that. Sometimes you can name the speaker; sometimes the other person can refer to them by name in a reply, or in a question; sometimes you'll sneak clarity into your surrounding description. If all your speakers are of the same gender – even if you only have a pair of people who are the same gender – make absolutely sure that the reader can tell who is speaking.

Your aim should be to deliver a scene which you can, in your own way, feel is fully rounded, convincing and clear. A good dialogue scene can be packed with sneaky exposition (people have to explain things to each other), sneaky description (But everyone knows, John, you're a very attractive man, even if you don't think *so*), and a sense of characters bending close to the reader and being developed at speed and with intensity.

Endings

Romesh Gunesekera

New writers are often worried about the ending of their novel – after they have worried themselves into paralysis, and eventually out of it, about the beginning.

'How do I end it?'

'How do I know when I have reached the end?'

The answer is, you do know how and you do know when you have ended it. There is not much you can be sure of in a novel under way, but one thing that you will be sure of, at least for a little while, is that you have reached the end. There is a destination, and when you reach it you realize that you have done so. But the journey is not over. Your first reader will tell you that. 'What happened next?' Soon after you reach the end you also realize you can revise the journey. It is often only at that stage that you can tell whether you started in the right place. Or ended in the right place. If the beginning is right and the end is right, you will see the shape of the novel and be able to judge whether the middle is right.

One writer I met along the way explained it very simply. When she had finished her novel she showed it to her editor. The response was enthusiastic; the only suggestion was to revise the beginning as it didn't quite promise what was delivered at the end. So she revised the beginning and resubmitted. This time she was told the beginning was fine and very promising but now the end didn't quite follow and fell short of the promise. So she rewrote that too. But then the response was that the beginning and end were wonderful but the middle didn't connect the two. So she revised that and then discovered now the beginning was no longer right. . . . The end of this process of revision is less easy to discover than the end of the story. It can go on indefinitely. The best advice I have come across about when to stop rewriting and editing is when you discover that you are simply putting back and taking out the same things, over and over again. Sometimes the same words, sometimes just the punctuation, as in that Oscar Wilde moment he describes: 'This morning I took out a comma and this afternoon I put it back in again.'

We all do it, and it seems obsessive nit-picking, but the endless tweaking is not a sign of insecurity: often it is a perfectionist tendency or a desire to play, both of which are essential for a writer. The problem is not knowing when to stop and to move onto the next sentence, the next paragraph, the next scene or the next chapter. Or even the next book. Therefore it is worth having a rule that says when the same comma disappears and reappears three times, it is time to move on. Or have a deadline when play must stop. If neither of those works, you will need to get someone to walk in and take your manuscript/typescript/computer away from you.

Perhaps all three will happen, and the writing and the rewriting will end. But have you reached the end of the novel?

This is for you to decide and there are no rules to apply. No tell-tale signs either. All you can do is ask yourself a few questions and see whether that gives a clue.

Is the main story there, or are you still at the preamble?

– It is a common problem that the first third of a novel is no more than the limbering up of the writer preparing to start the novel, then another third that turns out to be a leisurely, meandering journey setting the scene, getting to know the characters and exploring every uninteresting detail that caught your writerly eye, and then only in the final third does the panic set in and the whole story is told in a rush.

Has there been a journey of any sort between A and B?

– I don't mean the characters need to jump into a Chevy (or a Hudson, to be strictly accurate) with Sal and Dean, and go on the road from Patterson to San Francisco. By journey I mean some movement, physical or mental. In other words: is there a beginning and an end? Has anyone walked from one side of the table to the other, or gone from one thought to another? One can of course be experimental or avant-garde, which may be a little passé now, but if it pleases you, you can do it. The beginning and the end could be interchangeable. You could have a novel that reads forwards, or backwards or both. But in all cases there has to be some movement. Or, as in the next point, you could just ask:

Has something happened?

– Pure static. White noise. Blank pages. These are all O.K. and fun and maybe artistically interesting, but since Laurence Sterne did it all with *Tristram Shandy* in 1759, these gimmicks gain nothing in repetition. And of course a lot happens in *Tristram Shandy* between the marbled pages, the black pages, the blank pages. I think too much happens along the way, which makes it difficult to get to the point of completion.

Is there a sense of completion?

– The sense of completion needs to be felt in the reading, not the sense of relief in finishing the writing! When the reader gets to the last paragraph, it can come as a surprise, especially on an e-reader. But once we get over the shock of leaving the world of the novel, does it feel that the story is complete? It needs to feel both complete and paradoxically incomplete, as we want the story to continue beyond our reading. See the next point.

Can the story continue? Does it have room to grow?

– Novels, even if tightly plotted and neatly knotted at the end, need to give a sense that the lives in it will continue. Even if all the characters are dead at the end, something in that world of the novel needs to seem to continue and have an independent existence.

Has what was promised at the beginning been delivered by the end?

– We all make rash promises at some point. Novelists make very rash promises at the beginning of a novel. In the opening pages the reader is invited to enter a new world, to follow the story, and to be guided by a voice that promises to tell you things you never knew, or never knew you knew. By the end of the novel the reader needs to feel that it was worth trusting that voice.

Have you fallen short of the finishing line?

– The novel is done. There is no more to tell. The trouble is you can see the finishing line is yet another 50 pages away. It happens when you are in a rush. You've been in such a hurry to get it all done that you've written the notes for a novel, or an overextended synopsis. In your eagerness to get it done and meet your deadlines and follow all the advice you have been given, maybe you have rushed the end.

Have you finished the same book that you started with?

– If it is a different book, it is not a disaster. The situation is retrievable. Some amputation and clever surgery will produce a new book that is possibly better than the one you had intended to write. In some ways it is only natural that you will finish a different book. It may have started 3 years ago, or 5, or even 10. You are no longer the same person you were when you started. The world is no longer the same place. Your novel may have started before the Internet, before mobile phones, most certainly before some other amazing technological change, whether it is 4G, or Google glasses or spacewalks. The chances are, if it is read at all, it will be read in a shorter period, within weeks or months, or possibly days (unless you have written *À la recherche du temps perdu* or *War and Peace,* in which case you won't have the time to be reading this). In any case the reading of the book you have written will take place in a different world, and it has to survive in it.

You might want to ask some of these same questions of your favourite novels and see how they fare. You may be surprised to find that *Far From the Madding Crowd* or *Jane Eyre* or *The Great Gatsby* ends the way it does. Would you have preferred Hardy to have given Hencher a reprieve? A chance to be good? Would you rather Charlotte Brontë did not address you as 'dear reader' at the end and disrupt the dream you were in? And with *The Great Gatsby*, do you approve of Baz Luhrmann editing the last line of the book for his film, to make Nick Carraway less critical of the society he has been observing? What if Tolstoy had had that pang of anxiety and decided it was all too much and Anna Karenina should step back from the rail tracks?

If these what-ifs are as absurd as believing Mussolini ended up as a waiter in Hong Kong, or that Florence Nightingale became the prime minister of Britain, then you know the story got it right. Your version may only be fanciful and not make a better book, but it will tell you what kind of writer you are, and what kind of book you might want to write.

Life lessons

A. L. Kennedy

When people begin writing they can sometimes develop strange ideas about how they should dress or behave, as if wearing a particular type of jacket might affect someone's prose style. Some would-be writers retreat behind a notebook, and effectively cut themselves off from life in an attempt to control and record it. Sometimes simply paying attention will pay more dividends than any exercise, any pose or any complicated piece of psychological self-help. **Be in the world and pay attention** – it will teach you more than you will ever be able to pass on to your reader.

As you go through your days, there are some games, or disciplines, that you can follow, simply to increase your levels of awareness, until your ability to pay attention heightens and your interest in the world and in your ability to create new worlds moves on to deeper and broader levels.

Senses

Monitor your senses – which ones work most strongly for you, how they balance and on what occasions they surprise you, or are particularly active. Try and find time in the day to simply monitor the information reaching you, even in still times. Eat a meal while focusing particularly on sound. Spend time with people you like, enjoy yourself and then reflect – why do you enjoy them? Is it the sound of their voices, the sensation of familiarity or emotional comfort? Does their perfume make you feel better, even if someone else is wearing it? When you meet a new experience, travel, undergo an emotional extreme, bang your elbow, or see a good show – **pay attention**. Be present in the moment, so that you'll remember, and then you can thumb through the detail and see what strikes you. In this way a writer lives a detailed and rich life – whether he or she is a globe-trotting adventurer, or only has the view through a window.

Media

Reading great fiction to enjoy it, to delight in the way that it does its job, would be something I would hope you do as much as you can. (A disadvantage of writing fiction is that it eats into your time to read it). Speaking personally, I would hate it if the idea of myself as a writer ever intruded too much into the joy I get from reading, or if it made the process terribly self-conscious. But the world is full of other kinds of writing, ripe for you to pull it apart. It used to be that good, small newspaper articles were a great place to look at economy, working structure and a certain simplicity in the transmission of information. Now they're more likely going to offer lessons in how to obscure meaning by careless use of syntax, or how to peddle personal prejudice as fact – but lessons are always helpful. Look at the pieces that work, the profiles that give you a sense of someone – and at the gratingly obscure and self-obsessed, and see how truly annoying bad writing can be.

Advertising copy can offer similar assistance. Why does a slogan stay in your head? Why do you enjoy one little scene, why does another seem utterly offensive? What are the underlying human needs the seller is trying to excite? A good sales pitch is powerfully manipulative – fiction does its work in a different and hopefully more subtle way (most of the time), but don't let anybody's skill-set pass you by when it comes to the use of language.

When you go to see a movie, stare at some reality TV, go to the theatre, or come across a piece of TV drama – what's working and what's not? Are those lines really good, or is the performer making them good? Are those lines unsayable? Why doesn't reality TV seem real? What illusions best give the impression of real life? When material is cut interestingly, pushes pace in unusual ways, departs from convention to produce an effect successfully – can you transfer those techniques into your own work?

Within any given month

Read a new author.

Read a good children's book – not one of those intended for adults trying to retreat into infantilism, a really good one – and notice the power of pure storytelling in the best of that genre, that joy in creation that often falls away in adult fiction.

Visit an inspiration, giving it proper time – a walk in the woods, an hour with your grandmother, that art gallery tour you never got around to, an evening with all your favourite movies, favourite records, favourite people, favourite foods. Or pick something you feel you wouldn't enjoy – because I always assume I'll hate opera, I get a lot out of it when I do encounter it; and I always pay more attention to contemporary dance, even while I expect to be appalled. (Sometimes I have been delighted.) Take yourself to the aquarium, a cheese factory, a new part of town, the end of the bus route or the park you always walk by.

Talk to someone you don't know. Actually ask about them and listen to what they tell you. This doesn't mean you should steal her or his life and recycle it – just enjoy who they are, a small idea of the size of who they are. This can become habit-forming. Having a sense of the interior complexities and surprises of even unpromising-looking strangers can be hugely helpful when you catch yourself trying to get away with writing flat, bland characters.

Take one day – at least – absolutely to yourself to rest and reflect on what you have done in your work. Look at whether your writing habits could be improved, whether you're maintaining your health, whether you're resting enough, whether your life is in balance. If all is not well, try and make plans to adjust. If some matters are out of your control – convince yourself to avoid worry. Change what you can change, leave what you can't and go on as best you can.

Feel free to keep a diary or journal, but don't let it chain you to endless duty writing. A notebook may help you, but try not to expect too much of your notes. Make them fast and move on. There will be times when you want to perfect, say, a description included amongst notes in order to prove that you can, or with a definite aim in mind. But do remember that spending a lot of time cranking out prose that doesn't accommodate considerations of character, plot and structure – those pretty notes we all fall in love with at first – is basically forcing yourself to practice writing badly. Make a note that will help you write something properly later.

The poisoned chalice

A. L. Kennedy

Be careful, as they say, what you wish for.

When we start out as writers, it's not unlikely that we're simply doing what comes naturally, what fascinates and calls us. We work hard, because we're also having fun and satisfying ourselves – if not a local writers' group, or our captive relatives. We are doing something we love.

But, if we're serious about our craft, we do hope that will change. In fact, it would be dreadful to think that it wouldn't change. We are writers, we want people – usually – to read us. The more people read us, the more likely we are to be able to earn a living by writing. When we earn money by writing, we are buying time to write more. That's a good thing. But doing something about love, something which can be immensely intimate, for money . . . well, there's an ugly name for that. Not insulating our creativity from our commercial activities can leave us feeling exploited, insecure, even violated in many ways. The kind of writer who puts words on paper because delivering them to fellow humans in person would be traumatic may be further traumatized by dealing with the demands of agents and editors, rewriting and packaging their product. (Because to some people our dreams are simply products.) Almost any kind of writer may, at least sometimes, find it tricky dealing with the stage beyond that – the point at which the writer and the writer's work become public property.

Of course, we don't want our efforts to disappear, or for the mainstream media's ever-shrinking review space to find us indigestible. We don't want our novel never to be published. It wouldn't be ideal to launch it into cyberspace with inadequate editorial and marketing support and then watch intently as no one notices. We may not have started writing with the aim of being rich and famous, but issues of public exposure and commercial viability will enter in extremely quickly if our work prospers.

On the financial side, if you're writing literary novels, you're very unlikely to need specialist advice when your first advance comes in. It's not going to be a life-changing amount of money. The days when it was relatively easy to write novels for a living are probably over, unless you're fantastically lucky, hit a genre fiction mother lode, and/or suddenly win every prize out there on a regular basis. Simply bear in mind that if you're self-employed your life will probably be easier with a good accountant. Make sure they understand that an advance payment for something may mean your income is higher in 1 year and then crashes the next – when your tax is due. Make sure you set aside enough money to cover your liabilities. It used to be that one's advance money could gain interest in a standard savings account without being locked up inconveniently for years. Currently that's not the case. If you feel you're going to be unwise with your money, you can, with your agent, negotiate a reasonable payment schedule with your publisher and have small regular sums paid to you. And you can usually claim up to 50 per cent of your advance, genuinely in advance, should you be in trouble financially – although this would obviously reduce later payments.

A good agent and a good accountant will guide you through – that's why you pay them their fees. Don't be a scatty artist who ends up having to cough up decades' worth of tax and penalties because of non-compliance. I've seen it happen and it makes life utterly miserable for everyone involved.

Now to the public aspect of your life as a novelist. The novel is the 'big' form, if anything is going to get you attention, this will be it. Your publisher has a kind of obligation to help publicize your work, you have very probably signed a contract that contains a clause saying something along the lines of 'The author will undertake all reasonable activities to publicize the work.' And this will usually involve you in being publicized yourself. There's only room for one or two fascinating recluses in English-speaking literature – for this to be a practical position, your book/books have to be doing incredibly well without you and, frankly, until Thomas Pynchon dies (may this never happen) it's probably still not that feasible. So you will be asked to sit with journalists and be interviewed, perhaps to write personal pieces in the press, perhaps to appear at readings and festivals. This doesn't need to prove onerous or dangerous, but it can. And no one will really tell you what to watch out for. Learning by trial and error can be extremely unpleasant, but there are some points to remember.

Sitting in rooms talking about yourself for hours and even days at a time may well make you feel slightly insane. It may make your life seem unconvincing to you. It may mean you are rather odd around people who are normal and don't simply want a monologue from you about the wonders of yourself. There may also be a slight tension if you're being cautious, as you should be, about your own and others' privacy – a friend of mine talks about the long-term stress of 'not quite lying'. I don't know if there's any solution to this beyond becoming habituated, maintaining gratitude that anyone cares about your work and taking breaks when you can. Do try to remember that journalists are trying to do a job and be courteous to them, even if they're unpleasant or you're really tired and have had to talk through your lunch and have a reading pending for the evening. . . . It's part of the job, it's necessary, it's not as if you're felling trees, or mopping up blood and shit in a hospital ward. Just be gentle with yourself and try to detox with friends and family when you can.

Bear in mind that being in the media at all will mean that – on quite unpredictable occasions – members of the public may stare at you in the street, write you letters (both kind and crazed), talk to you as if they know you or get nervy and drop things around you. Again, you will get used to this.

Think of your career as a kind of prism through which courteous and rude behaviour becomes slightly magnified. People may give you things in shops. (Actor friends of mine get designer clothes, shoes, glasses, watches. . . . Writers are not generally that fortunate. I have received free vegetables and fruit in the past.)

Your friends may become wary around you. They may anticipate that you're going to become weird and grand. And if you do, they may find this unpleasant; I think that's fair enough. They may also find it irritatingly funny if you complain about the pressures of your new media-afflicted existence. If they really are friends, they'll stay friends – they'll know that sometimes everyone gets fed up with their job and they'll be there for you. Acquaintances, you may lose. Or suddenly people you barely know may want to get much more involved in your life. People who never liked you may take great care to say how much they hate your work – because now it's a kind of doorway to your heart. And people – generally, I find, men you don't know that well – will ask if such and such a character was based on them. . . . And you'll get used to all of this. Be kind, be courteous, be reasonable – and if someone else isn't, you have the right to go away and leave them to it. Be glad you are never going to have to deal with the rudeness, high-pressure scrutiny and insanity that actors attract.

The public

The first time someone asked me to sign a book, I actually said they were maybe mistaken in wanting me to. I didn't feel like someone who should do that kind of thing. (To be fair, the book in questions was an anthology and it felt a bit wrong to be scribbling at the front of a group effort.) Another writer involved, as the bemused reader drifted off, pointed out that it was my job to sign the bloody book and that I should go and call the reader back and get with the programme. Which I did.

Members of the public can be alarming. This may be because they are nervous of you – it's amazing how nervous people can get and for how many reasons personal to themselves, even if you've only written a short story in some throw-away collection by a small press. They can also be intense – they've had you in their head, they may think they know you, are your friend, or that you should always be in their head. Try to be calm. Try to be grateful they've turned out for you and bought your book – they are paying your wages. And try and enjoy them as people who are keen enough on books to attend events. Ninety-five per cent of the time, once you have conquered the general weirdness of being peered at and listened to as if you were someone of significance, then you can just have fun chatting with book lovers. Book lovers are some of the best people around. And if they came to your event, they like your books. How good is that of them? It's very good.

Don't feel bad about yourself if an event is oddly planned, impractically arranged, beset by technical difficulties and just generally shambolic – that's all down to the people who set it up. There's no point being in a mood with them, or with the audience – concentrate on making the time pass as pleasantly as possible. And remind yourself before the next reading, or workshop, or trip with an overnight stay that there are elements that you require to be in place. It will help if you say what those things are – whether it's a flip chart, or a mike that someone has tested, or a B&B that doesn't make you want to kill yourself. In my experience, the people who run events well will treat you well and the people who treat you badly won't pay any attention to anything you say beforehand. Other authors will know places it's good to avoid and places where you can go and have a lovely time, so check with them – there's a kind of informal rating within the community and it's rarely wrong.

Always carry a spare invoice note and keep a record of any agreed fee. Some people simply dodge paying at the end of the event and it's too late by then to do much about it.

Unless you hit the big time immediately, you will see an awful lot of pretty basic accommodation and/or stay in complete stranger's houses. This can be tiring if you have a run of cold, noisy, unpleasant nights. Try to check where you're going to be accommodated. If you insist on en suite facilities, that may slightly improve your lot. If you normally sleep naked and you're in the spare bed next to Granny's room and the bathroom is miles away, bring a bathrobe.

Eventually, you will develop a way of being with strangers. I find that concentrating on putting members of the public at ease produces ease for me. Usually, this involves taking an interest in them and being pleasant – as in the rest of life.

You may have to be pleasant to a great many people who aren't. But it's still wiser to be pleasant. If someone is only going to meet you once, try to ensure that they associate you with something good, rather than making them assume that you're going to be appalling for the rest of your life. And, should the chair for your event be rude/mad/drunk/otherwise unfit, try not to take it out on the audience. When you see a surly author, or panel of authors at an event with a chair you may well be looking at the result of some prior mishap backstage, working itself through to a conclusion. I once sat on a panel which had been roundly abused by its chair and we proved probably quite horrible to watch until the Q&A session for the audience at which point we may just have redeemed ourselves, but I think we should probably all have done better at trying to rise above things. Bear in mind that event chairs may be more focussed on their stage persona than what they can recall of your book, or may even sit on stage and simply read the puff copy on the book jacket in lieu of having prepared at all – best to smile and keep on keeping on.

Remember that, even if you have a run of wonderful events and torrents of praise for a week, or longer – you're still just you, the literary world is tiny and marginal – no one owes you anything. Professionalism will always serve you better than prima donna tantrums or – like one author I warmed up for – insisting that you don't like to go out and perform if the event isn't sold out. That kind of attitude tends to imply that you have attitude. And there's an informal network of information on authors, too – if you're tetchy, demanding, always stoned, or otherwise a hassle, after a while you won't get booked.

But grandiosity among authors is rare. The world of writers is generally quite democratic and cares about the things you probably care about – words, books, reading, stories, a clean bed and a nice bit of dinner. Your position as a novelist means you can be in the same room, or even on the same platform with writers you've always loved and that – once you've got over the shock – can be great fun. No author whose work you adore will be that upset if you tell them. Avoid telling people if their work entrances you less than completely. You can make great friends during your public duties, gain a sense of the audience that supports your work, get good advice and test drive your prose with a listening audience. Events abroad also hugely help you to gain translation, so even the cut price student-run tours may be worth it, even if the food is dodgy and the sheets dodgier.

Stalking

There is, of course, a darker side to relations with the public. Writers do seem to get a fairly high percentage of stalkers, perhaps because readers do have a very intimate and long-term relationship with our texts, perhaps because writing courses, workshops and some events seem to attract a little more than their fair share of the mentally frail.

Make sure that you have public liability insurance – you can get this through being a member of the Society of Authors, or from most insurance agents. If you're working with vulnerable people you may have to take it out and it's a good idea anyway. If someone sues you, having fallen over a chair on the way out of a one-to-one session about pages 56–78, then you'll be covered.

Residential writing courses and even teaching can mean that you're alone in a room with all manner of people you don't know from Adam. On the one hand, you want to preserve the writer's confidentiality as you discuss their work, on the other, you might want to leave your door open so that someone with a problem doesn't cause you a problem later.

Don't give out phone numbers, or email addresses, or your home address to people simply because they ask for them. Be very careful engaging in casual chat online with someone who may feel they are in an intimate relationship with you. If you're writing something you couldn't explain to your partner, your mother, your best friend and the police, then don't send the message. I know that seems obvious, but sometimes you may be taken unaware. I've had to move house to avoid two different stalkers and had police protection for a while against another – and I'm an obscure literary typist, not some media pin up. This area is just unpleasant, time-consuming and dangerous.

And – as we're all grownups – I would mention that having one night stands on tour is certainly something that happens, but it may not be any more wise than one night stands in any other context. And if you've granted yourself to an avid reader, you may be unleashing far more in the future than you can deal with. Some people enjoy having groupies in both senses of the phrase, but I've met an awful lot of writers who have regretted the consequences deeply.

If someone is stalking you, tell event and course organizers to look out for them, keep a diary of incidents, ask people to accompany you when that's possible and tell the police. There is a fair amount of support out there, although if things escalate you may find yourself unable to prosecute before you're actually harmed. It's best to keep safe, restrict access and back off fast if someone seems strange.

Interviews

When you speak to journalists try to remember that their pieces are, in a way, always about them – their work, their ability to do a job on time and in a manner that gets them more work – and maybe more about them than that. The fact that they're interviewing you doesn't mean that they are interested in you, like you, like your work, or haven't got a brief to write something damaging because that will be more interesting than yet another puff piece about a novelist. They may think you're great and have volunteered and lobbied to get the gig and talk to you – which can seem a little intoxicating and perhaps lead you to be incautious in print. Which is never wise.

Remember that whatever you say and however you say it the material your conversation offers will be cut back massively and therefore be distorted. Try to be clear, try to say what you mean in a helpful way. A journalist is a stranger with an agenda. You may try to make them less of a stranger and you certainly should try to defend yourself from their agenda if it seems toxic.

If they have a very fixed idea of how you write/are/work which isn't applicable to you, try to disagree only politely. No one likes to feel wrong. If they haven't read your book, or have skim-read it fast and much of it passed them by, try to take that in your stride – it's not your fault that their lives are unmanageable. If you disagree with something try and offer a way out for them, rather than a lack of information.

You don't have to meet anyone in your home if you don't want your fixtures and fittings to be analysed. Some features insist on examining where you live – you can either say no to that kind of thing, or limit the scope of their enquiries, if they make you feel uncomfortable.

Remember that if you conduct an interview over the phone the content will probably be very garbled. It's probably better to conduct that kind of short interview by email if you can.

Remember that if you mention anyone else who is still alive, your mention may not be a gift. Your reference to them if they're well-known will almost always be couched in sexual terms, or given a passionate/hysterical spin. If you do need to reference any type of friend you might want to protect their privacy and nod to them in a manner that lets them know who you mean, but keeps them comfortable. Or you may want to think through how you will talk about those you care for in a way that respects them and makes others do the same.

Remember you may well be sitting opposite someone who is desperately trying to work out what the hell they're going to do with their 1,000 words about you. So help a fellow-writer – without being their freak, slave, or stooge. Unless you feel okay about that kind of thing.

You can make your own decisions about whether partners, pets, friends or plants are pictured alongside you. Novelists aren't particularly hot media property, but sometimes these things do arise and you need only do what you feel will serve your work.

You will be given a persona by the press based on very few minutes and references to previous encounters with questioning strangers, spread over a number of years. . . . Try not to be trapped inside some kind of prison identity. It's probably not wise to accept encouragement to be controversial for the sake of it, or to create media shocks. . . . It can make for a gruelling life and the media who promote you will eat you, just as quickly as they praised you, if you're relying on them for profile, rather than generating interest in yourself due to some kind of identifiable talent. Just as not writing expressly for money tends to keep us free and articulate, not writing for attention does much the same to save our sanity and prose styles.

If you genuinely want to use any public visibility to promote a cause, or help a charity or to campaign, then I think that's legitimate. If we have better than average articulacy there's no reason why we shouldn't use it to what we feel are good ends. This makes it all the more important to engage with the media as honestly, smoothly and straightforwardly as possible.

It's not hard to prepare yourself for interactions with journalists by reading interviews, googling pieces written by someone you know is coming to speak to you, looking at how other writers have dealt with certain issues and deciding with those close to you how you are going to deal with intrusions into your personal life.

Whatever you do, don't relax at the end of what seems to have been a good session and say something foolish and off the cuff.

Never believe that anything is off the record.

I can personally recommend going by one's initials, rather than one's name. I did this to allow myself a sense of security within which to write. As it has worked out, I now have a name I am called while doing the slightly bizarre things demanded of an author and my own name for when I am living the rest of my life. I have found this hugely convenient, and cross-reference with other initial-users has confirmed the benefits of initialdom.

Other exposure and activities

Although publishers' publicity departments will try to get your work coverage, unless you are a fortunate exception among first-time novelists, you will have to generate a good deal of profile yourself. And publicists are always impressed by profile and will therefore give you more chances if you're already doing a little of their work. Some authors would say a lot. But others may be happy with their publicists.

Yours is probably living on a ghastly treadmill of ticket-booking, troubleshooting, co-ordinating and understaffing-related chaos. As usual, if you behave well and professionally and take an interest in his or her circumstances, this does no harm. And if you have a complaint, do voice it. There's no need to be a doormat, or continually fobbed off with dreadful accommodation or skewed schedules.

As an author, you might be supposed to spend your hours in tranquil solitude, studying, reflecting and scribbling. In fact, if you want to earn a living you will probably be trying to get work reviewing in print, on radio and on TV. You may end up presenting documentaries or essays. You may end up on stage in 20 different countries in the course of an average year, often doing the same old reading followed by a Q&A, but sometimes taking part in events so peculiar that they generate enough hysteria amongst all concerned to take flight. I have met authors who ghost-write for golfers, doctor scripts, produce advertising copy, do panel TV shows. . . . These activities can help your books, they can be fun, they can earn money, they can encourage people to give you free vegetables, or suits. . . . The ideal would be to live a life you can find comfortable in as many senses as possible.

So it's not unlikely (or half as exciting as you might assume) that you'll end up being not only a novelist, but a journalist, presenter, blogger, Twitterer, performer, academic and public person of letters. None of this needs to be a dreadful problem, if you're doing things you want to and find them as enjoyable as possible, if you prepare well for each particular task and take advice from people who have been there before you.

Other writers

Interactions with other writers will be a great joy for you – they will provide advice, support, understanding and humour precisely when you really need it. My writer friends are among the most precious I have. But bear in mind that there will always be a small number of people who believe that you're overrated, more successful than you should be and a hollow shell of a being deserving only of contempt. You will come across writers who have decided to hate you on principle and they will be as bitter and unpleasant as they can, as often as they can. Try and allow that to be their problem. If you are genuinely doing better than they are, you aren't going to meet them that often. And – as someone once told me – *if they're stabbing you in the back it means you're out in front of them.*

Petty tiffs and matters of ego aside, the community of writers is a good one. It tends to care about worthwhile issues, to be generous with its time, to be funny and articulate, to always tell you when there's a book out there that you should read and to always remind you that what you do is valuable and should have dignity.

Saying no

A. L. Kennedy

I'm writing this piece to you now in this book about writing novels because, when I was asked to, I didn't say 'No'. I could be working on my novel, which is waiting in the back of my mind and biting my interior furniture to remind me that it wants to get underway again – and yet I am writing this instead. Because I didn't say 'No'.

On this occasion, I had very good reasons to not say 'No'. I think it's good to try and give something back to the writing community, particularly when it has been so kind to me and when the vocation has been such a generous presence in my life. I like and respect Romesh Gunesekera and this seemed a lovely chance to collaborate on something worthwhile with him. I knew I was going to be starting a novel while I wrote pieces for this book (about, among other things, starting a novel), and I hoped that these essays would help to focus me on the task ahead. And the guest contributions have given me the pleasure of sharing other writers' experiences of the novel.

These are all good reasons. The hopes that a piece of work will be pleasant to me, will be likely to help me grow in some way and may be useful to others – these are factors that speak in favour of accepting a commission.

But.

A great many writers – and I am among them – will spend a great deal of their working lives fighting to save time to actually do the work they care about most and which will reward them most deeply – the work at the core of their lives. Why? Because of the absence of 'No'.

Why the absence? Well, again, there are good reasons for it.

When we begin as writers, we are usually so delighted that we've received a commission, and we just run with it as best we can. Why wouldn't we? I spent the first 5 years of my would-be writing life desperately hunting about for gigs as a theatre reviewer, a bodice ripper reviewer (if there is such a thing) and a researcher for another author who routinely handed over his copy as my own. (He got paid, I didn't.) All of this gave me experience (mainly of stress and penury, but never mind). I learnt how to deal with deadlines and how to organize what little time I had for my own work, so I could do it as well as possible when I got the chance. It's no coincidence that my first book was a collection of short stories, with a fragmented and slim novel to follow. I was doing my best, but I was being pulled apart by the demands of a more-than-full-time job, a dodgy relationship, extreme tiredness and that anxiety which seems often to plague people who think they might be creative and who are therefore turning themselves inside out to find a sign that might confirm their suspicions.

In short, I was terrified of saying 'No', because people could go anywhere else and get someone better than me to do whatever was required. And I really needed the tiny amounts of cash which sometimes tumbled in as a result. And I really needed to be visible as a writer – any kind of writer – so that I could move forward into what I (slightly, almost) allowed myself to think of as a career.

And personal factors intervened. They tend to.

Although I was an exceptionally selfish young person, I couldn't say to my mother or my grandparents, 'I just can't make the time to travel and see you any more – I need to write.' Even I knew that would be a horrible thing to suggest. And when my partner – also a writer – read me his latest chapter over the phone and I tried to stay awake, I gave precedence to his work over my own, because I didn't want to end up having a fight. (And – quietly – I enjoyed the increasingly clear awfulness of his work. It made me feel better about my own.) I didn't return the favour – I didn't at all want to trust him with my writing. (If you ever want to know if you really should be in a relationship and you're a writer, ask yourself – *would I let them read my work?*)

And then there was that job – I worked in community arts and everyone I served was in a dreadful position and needed support and ideas and how could I not try to work something out for them that would be a bit helpful? Some of the people I worked with were dying − fast − and that gave them priority, even over my ego-driven fantasies of ever being published. I was putting in 60- and 70- hour weeks, and that was paying my bills, but also destroying most of the time I would have to put words on paper. On the plus side, I met a huge number of people, was exposed to a vast range of life experiences and saw contact with the arts, or practice of the arts, transform people in extraordinary ways. Individuals, families, institutions and whole neighbourhoods would find things they could make and own and be happy about and share with others. People found hope and companionship and careers. So, even when I was downhearted about my own access to the arts, I certainly couldn't doubt that they had the capacity to improve my lot, and that pursuing my blurry dreams was something that mattered. In the rather strained decade that followed, that faith was important.

As I gained a foothold as a writer, I tried to keep the standard of my work as high as I could, while also trying to reach out into unfamiliar areas. (Every area was unfamiliar at first.) This involved a good deal of slogging, and a slow transition from non-writing work that stopped me producing prose fiction, to other-writing work that stopped me producing prose fiction. Have I moved beyond that stage? Not really. Advances have shrunk, the cost of living has risen − I still, like many writers, have to juggle the ability to support my craft, the ability to pay my bills, the work I do because it may open doors I really want to walk through, the work I do as a favour, the work I do in support of things I care about, and the work I drift into because I wasn't feeling strong when someone pestered me to come up with it. Unless I win the lottery (unlikely, because I don't play the lottery) or some other financial miracle happens, this situation will very probably continue. Only the last category of work − the things I am pestered into − is entirely expendable. The others must be managed sensibly, balanced and explored on a day-to-day basis.

But I would say to anyone who wants to be a writer that the art of saying 'No' is desperately important. This is not only because it makes time for you and your work, and maybe you *could* just scrape by without that extra hundred quid − just for now − if instead you could nail the middle of the novel. Maybe a short-term loss could be a long-term gain. Thinking about saying 'No' allows you to begin learning to prioritize in a way that will keep you and your skills and inspirations safe. And it means you will still have time for the people you love. Sometimes. And the other things you would like to do. Eventually.

The other thing about being able to say 'No' is that it frees you at a fundamental and a philosophical level. If someone comes along and offers you wonderful money to do something horrible – it's magnificent to be able to tell them to go away and stop trying to ruin your life. If you know that going about your business in a way that suits other people but not you would not only be unpleasant, but bad for your work – then you can say 'No'. If you can be sure that, when it really matters, you're going to keep hold of your soul and maintain your sense of self as a writer – and not compromise anyone else's work, either – then you can keep your working life in good shape for as long as you want to be involved with it. You can actually make decisions that are designed to allow you to develop as a writer. And you can leave room for all those pleasant occasions when you would like to say 'Yes'.

Part 2:
Tips and tales – guest contributions

Tips from Novelists

In this section we have brought together an international range of novelists with their advice on writing. Most of the pieces have been specially written for this book, but a few have been adapted from published essays and interviews.

Hanan al-Shaykh

Hanan al-Shaykh is one of the most acclaimed writers in the contemporary Arab world. She is the author of seven novels, two plays, a collection of stories and a memoir of her mother's life, *The Locust and the Bird*. Most recently she published *One Thousand and One Nights*, a re-imagining of some of the stories from the legendary *Arabian Nights*, performed in Toronto and Edinburgh in 2011. Her work has been translated into 28 languages. She lives in London.

'You're a bee,' a neighbour said to me, when I was a young girl in Beirut.

'Me? A bee? Do you mean that I sting people?'

'Yes, bees sting, and bees know everything!'

It all started when I was climbing up the stairs in our building. All of a sudden I saw, through the window of the ground floor flat, that the cupboard was moved aside, and the door behind it, which separated the adjoining flat belonging to another family, was left wide open. The secret was out in the open, the mystery was resolved. Abu-Mahmood, our distinguished neighbour, father of five children, was having an illicit love affair with the woman who lived in the adjoining flat. They used the splendid opportunity to be together during the day, after his family left Beirut to spend the summer months in the South, and the woman's husband was away at work from early morning to the evening.

The news of the scandal spread like wildfire, and all the blame was put on my tiny shoulders, although I meant no harm to any one when I went knocking at every door, spreading the news of the cupboard and the open door, asking questions, arguing that yes it is my business, refusing to shush, blaming everyone for not being willing to expose the truth.

I learnt after that incident how important it was to put down on paper all my observations, my thoughts, my confusion, and what people talked to me about, or told each other when I was lucky enough to overhear their conversations.

My grandmother and other women of her age told magical tales and stories rooted in reality, sometimes in striking proverbs – 'You're slick enough to tailor knickers for a fly' or – when persuading me to eat more, since I was extremely slim, and uninterested in food – 'If you don't fatten up, you're going to stay as tiny as a flea's cunt.' And the angry Fatima who threw her husband's trousers away when he handed them to her as she was washing the family clothes in the communal gardens: 'This will teach you to take them off only when they're due to be washed!'

It was such a relief to discover a few years earlier that anyone can hold a pencil and write, and that books did not exist on their own, like trees, birds and water, as I once believed, seeing my father trembling like a feather whenever he held or read the only book we had at the house, the Quran, with its mangy pages and its black letters with intricate shapes.

I learnt to express myself and write about my feelings very openly – like the time when I visited my mother in the mountains. My mother had divorced my father, and had then married another man. I was taking a shower when I heard her singing in her beautiful, tender voice. I felt that I wanted to register those unusual feelings of warmth and happiness which engulfed me, wanting them stay with me forever.

In my journey to seek the truth I learnt to look out for others who expressed themselves in silence, with telling eyes, or with deep sighs. I would sharpen my observations, prick up my ears and examine the tone of voice, in order to be sure if I was hearing a lie or not.

Little did the neighbour who called me a bee know that one day I would become a writer. Yes, I am a bee, equipped with two wings, antennas, pockets to collect the nectar, baskets to collect pollen, and I shouldn't forget to stress that I am blessed with a tongue, five eyes and a nervous system.

My mind lifts me in the air to roam, to stop when I find exotic plants and flowers, bushes and humble nettles. I choose and disregard, choose time and time again. Yes, I have to be precise, because sometimes I have found myself buzzing after a scent, believing that it was going to lead me to the nectar, only to discover to my dismay and disappointment that I was following a mirage, a hairspray, a perfume from a bottle or a bar of soap. On those occasions I would disregard all the pages I had completed.

Nectar is quite evasive, it stores itself in the place one would least expect it to be – for example, in the sand, as I discovered when I had to go and live in Saudi Arabia in the 1980s. The nectar wasn't dew drops but a shock. The seed of a novel had planted itself in me, as soon as I stepped into the desert airport and the hot air blew in my face and I saw men in long white robes trying to ignore the presence of women, and when I found no sign of women except those shrouded in floating black robes.

I would dig my tongue deep down until I tasted the right nectar, my subject, from life and mankind and from the inner regions of my brain and heart. I did that before I began to worry about prose, images and style. I would take refuge in the beehive, living on my nectar, not wanting to venture out, worried that I would become dehydrated while my antennae collected and enabled me to choose from the abundance of conflicts, feelings, calamities, cries, laughter, arguments, secrets, the terror of actual wars and the private, personal wars which exist within us. The endless changes or stagnation in society, exile, love and ecstasy, endless uncertainty, truth or its opposite, not forgetting the question of life and death. I find myself in order to construct and build my honeycomb, feeding my thoughts, discarding unwanted episodes and characters who are unable to grow or to metamorphose. Yet, seeing the honeycomb complete in my hands, I never stopped to ask, how did this happen? How did all the ingredients combine at once? Was there a link between a certain vein from my guts and heart to my brain, stretching itself to my neck, down to my shoulder, right arm, wrist, palm and finally my fingers? Or is it all the doing of the white paper and my pen only?

When my first novel *Suicide of a Dead Man* was published in Beirut when I was 21, my illiterate mother commented: 'Great that you've decided to write stories rather than becoming a lawyer! For what is life about other than stories? From the day we open our eyes, indeed, from the second we are born is the first story, and then the story of Adam and Eve, the Stone Age ancestors, history is a bunch of stories, not forgetting either the stories in every religion. If we disregard them than we don't believe in our existence.'

And I find myself answering her just now: my dear Mother, the world without stories and bees would cease to exist.

Bernardo Atxaga

Bernardo Atxaga is a Basque writer. His novel *Obabakoak* was awarded the Spanish National Literature Prize in 1989. His books have been translated into 32 languages. His most recent novel in English is *Seven Houses in France* (Harvill Secker, 2011).

WRITING NOVELS

Every novel needs a centre or a nucleus that influences and gives meaning to all its various elements. When everything is working as it should, when the characters, dialogues, tone, descriptions and even the punctuation are all operating under the hegemony of that one centre, a reader usually has a sense of harmony and unity, a feeling that there is neither too much nor too little of anything. I remember asking a reader to tell me what Carson McCullers' novel *The Heart is a Lonely Hunter* was about, and he said: 'Well, basically, it's about how the heart is a lonely hunter.' He meant that the novel's 80,000 words were a response to that single poetic idea around which they orbit just as satellites, asteroids or solar dust orbit around a planet.

Sometimes, the centre of a novel is clearly visible, as in the case of novels that belong to a specific genre – detective novels and thrillers, for example. Where is *their* centre? To find their defining elements we have only to look at the shelves where we keep our copies of Agatha Christie, Georges Simenon, Dashiell Hammett, Patricia Highsmith and other such authors. Could these novels exist without the police, without detectives, without a crime (or even two or three) to set the narrative wheel turning? Well, anything is possible in the world of literature, but that would be most unusual. The difficulty for a writer who wants to follow that route is not so much finding a centre for his novel as finding a gap on the shelves by making his protagonist stand out in a universe overpopulated with detectives or by setting his chosen crime in the context of some new social reality. In that sense, it's likely that the traditional homeland of detective fiction – namely, the English-speaking world – will tend gradually to diminish in importance. I'm no prophet, but I predict that the next famous detective will be Chinese.

If, however, the author wants to turn his back on such genres and write out of his own experience, his own imagination, his own personal orbit, the search for that centre will be a lot harder. He'll need to do more than just give a peremptory glance at the books on his shelves. He'll have to ask himself questions such as 'What voice do I write in?' Or 'What subjects, what rhythms, what tones are original and exclusive to me?'; the kind of questions that were once popular at religious gatherings: 'Where do we come from?' Or 'Where are we going?'; questions that could take a whole lifetime (or even two or three) to answer. Indeed, there is a profound connection between the act of writing and the process of gaining self-knowledge and, incidentally, adding to other people's knowledge of human nature. It is, as I say, a difficult business.

According to Bernard Shaw, while everyone is always very free with their advice, they're much less willing to part with their money, which only proves, by pure logic, that advice is worth nothing. I am, nonetheless, going to make a practical suggestion. When it comes to finding the centre of such a novel, I think the best approach is to write the first ten pages as quickly as possible, then stop and read through what you've written. Do the adjectives that have cropped up along the way give some clue as to the tone? Is a character beginning to take shape? Is there a clear rhythm? Is there one particularly powerful passage? No? Nothing? The best thing then, as with an unsuccessful game of cards, is to shuffle the pack and deal again, that is, quickly write another ten pages and repeat the whole process. If the material looks more promising, then start editing and making changes, before launching into page eleven. Otherwise, start all over. And so on for 3 months. If nothing comes of this process after 3 months, the best thing any writer can do is to look for that elusive centre among the books on his shelves and start writing a genre novel.

To conclude: a second piece of advice. Engaging in manual tasks is often very helpful to a writer. Robert Graves talked about how he used to do the washing-up and the laundry. It's not a bad idea and can prove interesting. And at least the family will be pleased.

Translated by Margaret Jull Costa

Tash Aw

Tash Aw is the author of three novels, which have been translated into 24 languages; the most recent is *Five Star Billionaire*. His work has won numerous prizes and twice been long-listed for the Booker Prize.

I seem to have become one of those writers I used to laugh at – the ones whose precious sensibilities demand self-imposed social exile in order to write, the ones who take themselves off on 'retreats' to work on a couple of chapters. I used to wonder what they were retreating from, for the act of writing seemed to me inextricably linked to the act of living an everyday life: to separate the two seemed unachievable and unnecessary. I wrote most of my first novel while sharing a cramped basement flat in London – at night, when I wrote, wailing cats copulated in the air well outside my room and sometimes, as I lay awake in the small hours of the morning mulling over a character sketch or plot detail, I would listen to the never-ending traffic on the motorway a few hundred yards away. I used to love the noise, the colour and banality of urban life. My work was, and is, about the noise and grime and wonder of the human condition, so I needed to be close to it.

But times change; technology changes. I have always been easily distracted – and that, sadly, has not changed. Broadband internet was the big game-changer, the one thing that changed me from a writer who could write amidst the grime of city life to one who needed to *retreat*. Now I realize that the term is misleading. It isn't to do with fleeing anything, but rather finding something – my sense of myself as a writer, as a human being who can figure things out and think in a cohesive manner without the aid of a bunch of machines. I realized this when, one day in the middle of my second novel, I had exhausted all internet search possibilities: there was simply no more trivia for me to Google, nothing else I needed or wanted to know, no more books I had to buy on Abebooks, no other library database I could consult. I remember staring at the screen, my fingers poised to type something that I was certain would change the fortunes of my research. 'Memoirs of a Sulawesi Sperm Whale Hunter, 1870s,' I eventually typed, vaguely recalling the title of a book I'd seen in the British Library catalogue a few days earlier. The resulting search came up with nothing that made sense (my novel was set in Jakarta in the 1960s). I sat there, exhausted and bewildered. The list of nonsensical websites on the screen reminded me of something I had forgotten: the act of writing required, basically, only me.

These days, I find that a writer's retreat involves, quite simply, turning off my devices and checking my emails only once a day, or sometimes not at all. This may take place in a rural setting or in my flat in London, but wherever the geographical location of my retreats, the aim is always to strip away the layers of distraction that surround me in order to regain a mental and emotional space that allows me to feel alone. In this state of solitude, the fragments of information in my head begin to settle, crystallizing into something more solid and consistent. I don't mean that I am totally cut off from the rest of life – evenings are almost always spent having a quiet supper with friends, or out at the cinema – but for 6 or 7 hours a day, starting at 6:00 a.m., I don't engage with anyone other than myself. The longer I spend in this space, the freer I feel.

Joan Brady

Joan Brady was the first woman to win the UK's Whitbread/Costa Book of the Year Award. She has also won France's Prix du Meilleur Livre Étranger and a US Endowment for the Arts grant, and was long-listed for the Orange/Bailey's Prize. Her novels include _Theory of War_ and _Bleedout_. Her latest, _The Blue Death_, was the _Observer_'s Thriller of the Month.

A friend in my Pilates class gave me an article from the _New York Review of Books_ that said half of all Americans have gone to a university, and half of today's half are enrolled in creative writing courses. All these courses teach the same three rules for fiction. I've forgotten two of them, but the third sticks in my mind because it's puzzled me for years: 'Write about what you know.'

Where does such a rule leave Terry Pratchett? Or Mary Shelley? Or practically every writer of science fiction and fantasy? Where does it leave _me_? I danced with the New York City Ballet and wrote about how I got there, but that was a memoir. How could a gently brought-up woman like me possibly know anything about the subjects I've chosen?

My first novel. . . . The only comment I feel comfortable with is that it was *not* about a gently brought-up woman. The second, *Theory of War*, grew out of a family story. I'd paid no attention to it as a child but, middle-aged and casting about for a subject, I remembered my father saying that his father had been a slave. A slave? Really? But I'm white. So was he. Now that's interesting.

The Civil War that emancipated black American slaves was very bloody. It killed over half a million men, crippled many more, widowed thousands of women. No veterans programme. No war pensions. A high birth rate. How to feed all those mouths? In the meantime, farmers needed labour to work their land. No more black slaves and no machines, not back then. Children have small fingers, perfect for weeding; so it was a simple matter of supply and demand. The Norris family of Ohio – tobacco farmers – paid a veteran $15 for my 4-year-old grandfather; they housed him with the animals, worked him dawn to dusk, beat him until he bled, deprived him of an education.

Too good a story to pass up. But I know absolutely *nothing* about lives like that.

I looked for a nudge. Any kind of nudge. And I thought, what the hell, there's a sense in which every woman knows what it's like to be spat at. Admittedly flimsy – very flimsy – but a nudge. My grandfather won me the UK's prestigious Whitbread/Costa Book of the Year. I wrote a couple of thrillers about a heavily-muscled, violent, angry murderer who grew up in prison. I know nothing about murderers. I know nothing about prison. But who hasn't ached – however fleetingly – to kill? Who hasn't chafed at an unfair world? That's knowing *nothing*, the rule makers would say. But I made a lot of money.

What *I* say is that fiction writers are like God: we make something out of nothing. Somerset Maugham put it another way. He agreed that there were three rules for writing a novel, but he knew the score, and he went on to say, 'Unfortunately nobody knows what they are.'

Amit Chaudhuri

Amit Chaudhuri's fiction has won the Commonwealth Literature Prize and the *Los Angeles Times* Book Prize, among others. His first novel, *A Strange and Sublime Address*, is included in Toibin and Callil's *Two Hundred Best Novels of the Last Fifty Years*; his last, *The Immortals*, was a *New Yorker*, *Boston Globe* and *San Francisco Chronicle* Book of the Year. He is Fellow of the Royal Society of Literature, and was one of the judges of Man Booker International Prize 2009.

Writing novels is no fun; nor is, generally speaking, reading novels. Reading people writing about novels is not always fun, either, because relatively little of this kind of writing is any good. Then there's the group of people who don't enjoy being novelists, to which I probably belong; whose lives are at once shaped and defined by, and to some extent entrapped in, the act of writing fiction. I still find it difficult to believe that I'm something called a 'novelist'; but this hasn't stopped me from dreaming, frequently, of alternative professions: second-hand bookshop owner; corporate worker; cinematographer. There are many reasons for this unease. One of them is a fundamental discomfort with narrative itself, and involves admitting to yourself that you derive your basic pleasure not from knowing what happens next, but from arrested time or eventlessness; this makes you constantly wish, as you're writing, that you were elsewhere, or it makes you work to make the novel accommodate that impulse. Another reason is the professionalization of the vocation, so that the novelist is supposed to produce novels as naturally, automatically, and regularly as a cow gives milk. In such a constraining situation, money can certainly be a compensatory pleasure; so can that paradoxical and sly addiction, failure.

Stevie Davies

Stevie Davies is Professor of Creative Writing at Swansea University. She is a Fellow of the Royal Society of Literature and a Fellow of the Welsh Academy. Stevie has published widely in the fields of fiction, criticism and history. Her most recent novels are *Into Suez* (Parthian, 2010), and *Awakening* (2013).

EMPATHY AND CHARACTERIZATION

Empathic awareness is a foundation of realist fiction. But how can we abdicate our own agendas, to see through another's eyes? Empathy isn't quite the same as compassion, sympathy or pity, which relate to the misfortunes of others, 'over there'. Empathy seeks entry into the totality of the heart's labyrinth. Paradoxically, turning inwards in self-enquiry can offer a bridge. In *Middlemarch*, George Eliot ascribed 'spots of commonness' to Tertius Lydgate, idealistic doctor, tender husband, flawed human being. In Eliot's book, we all – writer, character and reader – exhibit versions of a common, and sometimes mortal, pathology. Studying myself, warts and all, can become a source of wisdom and insight.

For example, how do I realize on the page a complex character who, against the grain, acts cruelly? The straightforward answer is: through observation of others behaving cruelly in life. A readier way in is to examine my own cruel streak – how it felt to hurt someone; why I behaved in that way; the aftermath. A trove of rueful information is at once exposed. When George Eliot was asked to identify the model for her dessicated pedant, Edward Casaubon, she pointed silently to herself. I am guessing that she also resorted to forensic analysis of her own self-righteous tendencies to understand the brilliantly anatomized hypocrite Nicholas Bulstrode. Human blemishes and contradictions become tissue for analysis; microscopic self-scrutiny leads out into human nature. Gustave Flaubert is recorded as saying, 'Madame Bovary, c'est moi.' 'I am large,' writes Walt Whitman. 'I contain multitudes.'

A question novelists dread at festivals is, 'Is your central character based on yourself?' Yes and no. The author's self is diffused over the whole surface of a novel, in solution with the otherness of the world. The word 'empathy' comes from the Greek *empatheia* (affection, passion) via the German *Einfühlung*. It's related to our imitative capacities. To empathize I have to taste the experience of being you. I can start to do that from common ground.

Empathic power is never wholly comfortable. The sharp reader of the human face – who catches the nervous tic quivering at the eye, the weather in the face, the withholdings of a voice – can also be (like George Eliot's Dorothea Brooke emoting intensely over the breakfast table at her flinching husband) a raider. We hoard our secrets. Chekhov showed in *The Lady with the Lapdog* that the inner world can never be divulged or known – only guessed.

Empathy has limits. Sanity forbids, as Eliot reflects, a universal insight, for if we were alive to 'all ordinary human life, it would be like hearing the grass grow and the squirrel's heart beat, and we should die of that roar which lies on the other side of silence'. At its best, the limited empathy of which writers are capable can guide the reader into complex and obscure regions of the heart – like the surgeon's combination of miniscule endoscopic camera, light and microscope that secures a close-up view of intimate depths.

Anita Desai

Anita Desai is the author of *Fasting, Feasting, Baumgartner's Bombay, Clear Light of Day* and *Diamond Dust*, among other works. Three of her books have been shortlisted for the Booker Prize. Desai was born and educated in India and now lives in the New York City area.

FROM 'FLIGHT OF FORMS', AN ESSAY:

I suppose I began to write Fire on the Mountain when I was 8 years old and taken to Kasauli for the summer – even if I did not put down a word on paper then. At that time I was not the narrator of a book, but the source of one. That summer I was suspected by my mother of not being well or strong and requiring special attention; and was therefore kept mostly at home which was, for the summer, a large, square stone house on the hillside below the town. While my brother and older sisters roamed the upper ridges in search of adventure, I played by myself in the garden or wandered in the corn fields, the pine groves and apricot orchards immediately surrounding the house. Although I missed some grand and rather terrifying adventures, I believe it was because of this imposed isolation that I absorbed my surroundings, mulled over them and retained impressions at their most pure and vivid. I was not dissipating them by sharing them with anyone, nor diluting them by giving them only half my attention. The flash of a silvery *langur's* fur through the foliage, the odour of the dry pine needles on the hillsides and the feel of the stones and pieces of bark I played with in my solitary games sank into me indelibly: they sank in so deep that I lost sight of them and forgot them.

They stirred to life again when some 20 years later I found myself living in Chandigarh (that had not existed in 1945), and going up to Kasauli for holidays once more. This time it was my children who were exploring the hillsides, and through them I re-lived those earlier, almost forgotten experiences of sliding down a hillside slippery with pine needles, driving away a band of *langurs* that had descended on our zinc roof, gazing at the smoke from a forest fire and wondering if it would draw much closer. Like seeds that had been buried deep in the soil and stirred to life on feeling a shower of rain and the coming of the right season, the memories became living experiences once again.

While walking along the Kasauli Mall I would sometimes stop by the fence to look down the steep hillside at a small village below, its haystacks and cattle and stony paths, its small population of labourers going about with their backs bent under sheaves of grass, sickles tucked in at the waist. I wondered then if it was this village − or one nearby − where an acquaintance of my mother's had been done to death, a woman I had seen perhaps half a dozen times during my childhood, and since then quite forgotten. A spinster lady who taught, I think, in one of the women's colleges in Delhi, she had sometimes visited my mother in order to pour out her woes to a sympathetic listener. I am afraid she met with little sympathy from me. Like my father and brother and sisters, I found her tiny desiccated figure and astonishingly loud, braying voice utterly ludicrous and would run away, choking with laughter, when I heard her voice ring out at the gate. She was afflicted with a voice no one could bear; I doubt if she had any friends. Later, she left Delhi; my mother told me she was involved in a village near Kasauli. I think we received a few letters, telling of her hardships, her lack of money and her inability to do anything for the ignorant and stubborn villagers. Still later, the news came that she had been brutally assaulted and murdered by a villager, who resented her presence and her proselytizing. We were shocked. Then we forgot. She faded away.

On leaving the north and moving to Bombay, I felt the need to recapture that landscape which seemed essential to my survival − if I were not to die from the onslaught of a great and abrasive city, its unrelieved ugliness, squalor and noise. I sat down at my desk and set myself to recreating the sounds and smells and sights of the Kasauli hills. It was my belief in an experience of the magic power of words that made me feel I could do so through an act of intense concentration – that would have to replace my actual presence there. To do so, I had to send my 8-year-old self out into the hills again, wearing a straw hat that had slipped onto my back and chafed my shoulders, my feet in open sandals feeling the white dust and stubbing against the stones again. That child, its solitude, became the focal point of the book.

I had experienced that summer and those hills in solitude, and solitude became its natural theme. Although I had lost that sense of isolation on later holidays there, I recalled a woman who used to live on top of the hill above the cottage we rented, a Mrs S., whom I had not known personally but knew of and whose grey melancholy presence had struck me greatly. I used to see her going for solitary walks . . . occasionally on passing her house, I heard her playing her piano, meditatively and compellingly. I was later told of her sad death in solitude that she seemed to have willed upon herself. She joined the small sunburnt child straying on the hillside, as the second of my two characters.

Then, I was half-way through my book, still trying to discover why these two characters – the melancholy grey lady and the cricket-like child – were where they were, when I saw a grey, indistinct figure looming over the horizon, as insubstantial as a wisp of smoke from a forest fire. For a while, I could neither recognize it nor understand its presence in my book. Then, when I started to describe it, I gave a start of astonishment as I recognized Miss R. It was her ghost who had climbed up the hillside onto the Mall: I heard her voice ring out, shattering the silence that enclosed my two characters, in a scream for attention. In my state of shock, I forgot to laugh; in fact, I found I could not laugh any more; I saw now that she was not laughable at all, she was tragic. Although she had played a minute, indeed minuscule role in my life until then, and I had not thought about her in 30 years, she must have remained buried in my subconscious. To lay her ghost, to exorcize her unspeakable past, it was necessary to write about her. My memory of Miss R. was flawed; I saw her and remembered her from the viewpoint of a child unwilling to give her any time or sympathy – I was not capable then of either. It was therefore necessary to go back to my spare memories of her; attempt to understand and picture her wretched existence and unthinkable death – in order to arrive at what seemed to be the truth.

Jean Malquis: *The only time I know that something is true is at the moment I discover it in the act of writing.*

Norman Mailer: . . . *it is at this moment of intellection, this moment of seizure when one knows it is true.*

These characters could not exist in a vacuum; they could not float in space. They had to be provided with a background, and it had to be so real that it could be touched, heard, and felt. Kasauli provided that: sitting in a flat in Bombay and looking out over the slums smothered in city smog, I was nevertheless in touch with a different landscape, sunburnt and stark . . . words spun the threads that led me back to it, words were the bridge and became the web. The landscape could not possibly be just a background; it was too powerful to be merely that. Surely that twisted pine tree with two branches like out-flung arms against the sky had some meaning . . . the kite floating on currents of air through the gorges and silent chasms was symbol of some mystery that I could not understand, but invited me to delve into it and discover its significance, or at least proclaim its presence.

There were other elements that went into the making of the jigsaw puzzle, some vague and others definite: the element of terror that is never absent from even the most sunlit places of childhood (Flannery O'Connor: 'Anybody who has survived childhood has enough information about life to last him the rest of his days.'). The works of the Pasteur Institute that I heard as a child, and were connected with the horrors of snake-bite and rabies and became very real when we later lived in a cottage that overlooked the gorge into which the Pasteur Institute emptied its chutes, from which we could see its prison-like walls and its blackened smokestacks. . . . A night-time walk down a shadow-patterned road when we children tried to terrify each other by telling ghost stories . . . the small white graves overgrown with grass in the small British cemetery. . . . Also the impression, a lasting one, made on me by Mrs Ramsay in *To the Lighthouse* and the clinging charm of Sei Shonagon's *Pillow Book*. . . . The writing of the book became a curious mingling of the real and the remembered and the imagined – as every novel is. It is, after all, as E. M. Forster said, 'won by the mind from matter' and contains elements of both. The two can be seen as locked in combat or in harmony (W. H. Auden: *It is true that when he is writing a poem, it seems to the poet as if two people were involved, his conscious self and a Muse whom he has to woo or an Angel with whom he has to wrestle, but, as in an ordinary wooing or wrestling match, his work is as important as Hers'*) but the right proportions have to be found in order to balance the whole. If the book is to be strong, effective and meaningful, then the gaps between these elements, between the real and the imagined worlds, the objective and the subjective attitudes, the extrovert and the introvert elements have to be closed up; the two must mesh together, leaving no gaps through which credulity could drain. Having built oneself such a container, it might surprise one lowering it into those depths of memory, or swinging it through the free space of imagination.

Having pinned down my butterfly with my pen nib, I was not finished with it; I had still to see it through the press, correct proofs, finally be faced with the sight of it in a bookshop, available to all. . . . It had many incarnations; an English edition to begin with; then an American edition that carried the picture of a black witch on the cover; a paperback edition that displayed a bright hoopoe; a flyswatter and a landscape that never was; then translations in which I lost sight of the original, and that became originals in themselves. . . . It was read and received reviews. I was questioned about it. Readers were disturbed: what did it all mean? Was it a real fire or a symbolic one? Why did the child start it? Did the old lady die, or faint – 'or what?' Since I was responsible for it; I had to defend it. 'Don't you see?' I replied. 'Everyone in that book is living an illusion – their lives are built on illusions. To be rid of them, a fire had to be lit and only the child was pure enough to light it. Everything had to be burnt away in order to reduce it to ash and reveal the truth.' I was surprised by my own explanation: it had not occurred to me till I gave it that it was one. Certainly it was not my intention when I began to write that book but, to my relief, it fitted; it had been fortuitous but it had turned out right – one of those instances of stumbling upon the truth rather than pursuing and capturing it.

Louise Doughty

Louise Doughty is the author of seven novels, most recently the bestseller *Apple Tree Yard*. Her sixth novel, *Whatever You Love*, was shortlisted for the Costa Novel Award and longlisted for the Orange Prize for Fiction. She has also won awards for radio drama and short stories, along with publishing one work of non-fiction, the how-to-write book *A Novel in a Year*.

THE MUDDLED MIDDLE.

There comes a point during the writing of every novel where the novelist writing it experiences something akin to despair. Well, if you only have one point of despair, then you are getting off lightly – there are many, of course, but there is one that I find particularly bleak. It comes in the middle of writing a book, a phase one of my students once called 'the muddled middle', which is as good a term as any for the confusion that reigns in a writer's head some way past the starting point but a long way from the end.

The muddled middle doesn't actually have to consist of the middle of a novel, or only in the loosest sense of the word: it exists in the grey area past 10 per cent but before 90 per cent of your first draft. For me, it's usually around 30 per cent of the way in, when I have written a whole load of scenes, set a bunch of hares running, got past the initial enthusiasm for the idea and started to ask myself where on earth the book is going because it really, really has to start going somewhere soon. It is the stage where you have to follow through on all the things you've set up, the stage where you have gone too far into a book to abandon it but are still swimming around in a morass of ideas, thoughts, half-written scenes. . . . A novel at that stage is less than a half-formed thing, it is no more than the swirling collection of dust before the big bang. It is something that may be anything between one of the great works of twenty-first century literature and a complete dog.

In other words, you haven't the faintest idea what you are talking about – and if you don't work it out soon, neither will anyone else.

This is always the point at which I say to myself, 'hey, guess what, you've got away with it up until now, but this is when you get busted'.

As I write this, that feeling is more potent than ever. My current work – now labouring under its fourth working title, which I won't share – is the second in a two-book contract. The deadline is hurtling towards me like a runaway train. I have yet to miss a deadline in my entire career (and this is novel number eight) but hey, there's a first time for everything. A lot of novelists hate working towards deadlines but I like the adrenaline buzz and have always found the pressure productive, until now.

Recently, I realized there was only one solution to the despair I was feeling: run away. I mean this quite literally. I had written around a third of the new book but it was a morass of individual scenes, a very rough plan, a plot that spanned two decades and was set across three continents, a bulging plethora of research notes. The first two chapters were written and the final scene and the rest of the material was chaotically spread in between in states varying from finished prose to scribbled reminders torn from a collection of notebooks. It was a novel that was being not so much written as regurgitated.

So I said to my family, 'I'm going to Southend.'

'Why?' asked my partner. 'Southend is a dump.'

Southend is a seaside resort on the coast of Essex, England, and I'm now very fond of it and won't hear a word against it: dump it ain't, but Brighton it ain't either.

'I know,' I said, 'that's the whole point.'

Southend is easy to get to by train from my North London home – and it had a lot of out-of-season hotel room availability (this was February, mind). I went there for three nights, spread my novel out over the hotel room floor, sat back on my heels and stared at it.

It will seem odd to some that a novelist can go to the trouble and expense of holing up in a hotel room for 3 days and not write a single word: but those 3 days of staring at my book were absolutely essential. Sometime around the second day, I finally saw what I should have seen all along: that with a complicated time frame I had to narrow my geographical locations; that the main character had returned to Indonesia in the 1990s not in spite of what he had done there 30 years previously but because of it; that his life journey clearly bracketed the rise and fall of the Suharto regime; and that the novel was, amongst other things, about the moral complexity of the West's economic interests in suspect or repressive regimes. All this I knew, but I had to stare at the material for 3 days for it all to settle in my head, and for me to order my half-written scenes into a progression that made sense. Chapters One and Two are in the 1990s – and then it goes back in time to a large chunk set during the abortive coup attempt in the 1960s and the massacres that followed. I even saw where a vital flashback to the main character's childhood in California in the 1940s needed to go – exactly halfway through, since you ask.

So the middle still isn't written, but it isn't muddled any more. My character's darkest secrets have revealed themselves to me and I have decided when they should reveal themselves to the reader – all because I ran away and stared at it for a few days.

It's a process I can recommend, although it is possible you may be able to find a venue that is a little prettier and less chilly than Southend in February. Wherever you choose to run away to, I would wager that it is an unavoidable point in any novel's progress. I'm no further in, in terms of word count, and yet the muddled middle is behind me. The road ahead is long, but clear.

Anne Enright

Anne Enright is an Irish novelist, essayist and writer of short stories. Her work is globally translated and has won various awards including, in 2007, the Man Booker Prize. She lives in Bray, Co. Wicklow with her husband and two children.

I hit 50 this year and am surrounded by people who are also hitting 50. 'Hitting' is the word – you would think it was a wall and not a line in the sand. It is a time of reckoning, rather than of tweaking the mechanism, a time when we confront not just the wrinkles in the mirror but the fantasies once held by our younger selves. Ambition and fantasy have the same relationship as love and fantasy, or sex and porn. In the fantasy version of our lives books are written without effort and they become instant classics. Why is life not like this? Why is reality so difficult? I have no more interest in '50' than I have in '42 and a half': it is a number I am happy to ignore,

but if I do have a serious mid-life crisis, I will get a tattoo, and that tattoo
will read:

200
words
a day

This is my answer to all the questions I am ever asked about how to write,
and where do I get my ideas from, and how do I start or finish a book. This
is my answer to the fuss about writing books. It is all I know.

Jonathan Franzen

**Jonathan Franzen is the author of four novels, _Freedom_, _The Corrections_,
Strong Motion and _The Twenty-Seventh City_, and four works of non-
fiction: _Farther Away_, _The Discomfort Zone_, _How to Be Alone_ and most
recently, _The Kraus Project_.**

**This is an extract from an interview with Chris Connery recorded in 2009
and published in _Boundary 2_.**

Chris Connery: . . . _In addition to [your] novels, you have published a number
of important essays, including . . . a major essay on your ambitions as a
novelist and your relation to what has been called the social novel. This
essay, originally titled 'Perchance to Dream' . . . appeared in revised form
under the title 'Why Bother' in the collection_ How to be Alone.

Jonathan Franzen: One of the things I talk about in the essay that I prefer
to call 'Why Bother?' is the relation between the supremacy of the novel
in the nineteenth century and the fact that it had no major competitors.
It's not necessarily fair to measure our culture's engagement with political
reality by the health of the social novel, now that we have shows like
The Wire and now that we have CNN. . . . And yet it's hard for me not to let
my sadness about the decline of the social novel affect my judgments of
the culture as a whole. There's no question that the ambitious programme
of Proust, Dickens, Tolstoy and Trollope is simply not present in the same
way anymore. It's been transferred to a non-literary realm, and this is a big

loss, because the novel is the greatest art form when it comes to forging a connection between the intensely interior and personal and the larger social reality.

As for my own ambitions for the novel nowadays, I make fun of the ambitions I had when I was 22 and thinking, 'I will write the book that unmasks the terrible world, I will cause the scales to fall from the public's eyes, and they will see how stupid the local news at 11 is, and they will realize how cliché-riddled the pages of their local newspaper are and how corrupt their elected officials are. And they won't stand for it any more.' Exactly what kind of utopia I thought would ensue was never clear.

CC: *Well there's certainly something utopian in just capturing the social form itself . . .*

JF: . . .Placing an intensely individual character in dramatic and symbolic relation to large structures and large themes in the country I live in: this is where things start happening for me. This is what's fun. It's probably because, as a person, in real life, I can never check my own analytical and political side at the door. . . . I don't write about these things because I want to be a 'social novelist'. I do it because I can't ignore them as a person. Simply to do work that excites me and seems true to reality, I have to take the big picture into account. . . .

CC: . . . *What would you say the novel still has to do or still can do?*

JF: Well, I think you more or less just said it. We may just be little specks. . . . And yet, as you go through life, you still hit these points of crisis where something genuine is happening. A choice is being made, or a life is being destroyed, or hope is being regained, or control is being relinquished or control is being achieved. These moments may be utterly insignificant historically, but they're still hugely meaningful to the person experiencing them – as meaningful as everything else in the world put together. To try to connect with what might formerly have been called the soul, and what I might now describe as some interior locus of privacy and reflection where moments of personal significance are experienced: this, I think, is the job of the fiction writer. . . . I think these epiphanic moments have a social and political valence as well, because they're what we mean when we talk about being a person – about being an individual, about having an identity. Identity is precisely not what consumer culture says it is. It's not the playlist on your iPod. It's not your personal preference in denim washes. The moment you become an individual is the moment when all that consumer stuff falls away and you're left with the narrativity of your own life. All the things that would become impossible – politically, emotionally, culturally, psychologically – if people ever were to become simply the sum of their consumer choices: this is, indirectly, what the novel is trying to preserve and fight in favour of.

CC: . . .*You've written a few short stories, but you're not a short story writer. And you clearly have a commitment to the long novel. . . .*

JF: Short stories are very hard, actually harder than the novel. Occasionally I hit one right and it works, a little more frequently now than in the past, when they were always failures. . . . My experience of daily life, even hourly life, is one of constant conflict and division. Of simultaneously being never fewer than two and often as many as four or five different people. And I very much suspect that I will never succeed in writing a book with a single point of view (POV), a single character who carries the whole thing. . . . The novel to me is the venue for sympathy. In terms of leading my actual life, being a divided and conflict-riddled person is unpleasant. 'Disaster' would be too strong a word, but it's definitely no fun. At the same time, my psychic splinteredness does mean that there are few impulses in human beings that I don't have some way of connecting with. The novel to me is the art form that allows scope for my impulse to turn things around and look at them from another perspective. . . . [Also] there's a wish to have fun, often satirically, with a civic reality that I get bathed in simply by moving through the world, and you can't do that in a short story. It doesn't work. It really is like the difference between painting on a 12 foot by 12 foot canvas versus painting on a 12 inch by 12 inch one. Certain things become possible simply because of scale. . . .

CC: *You also have America, the US as your object. . . . [Your]characters exist along with this bigger vision of America. And that obviously can't go into a short story.*

JF: . . . Characters need space in which to reveal their complexity. Even though they're always simplified and cartoonish in comparison to a real person's character, they still have their own complexity. You need to give them time to really be themselves. . . . Plus I don't develop a really good character every day or every month or even every year. It's like making strudel dough. You stretch it out, you fold it over, you stretch it out, you fold it over. You do that about thirty times. It's a long process, and a character who's developed in this way doesn't really fit into a story. And then, having taken the time to develop four or five characters like that, you don't want to just burn them up in 20 pages. And, beyond that, I can't seem to write well about characters I don't love. Sometimes it seems to me that my defect as an American fiction writer is that I tend to be monogamous and form strong, loyal attachments. I don't want just a 2-week quickie with the character. I want to get into a 5-year relationship.

But, to go back to [your] question. . . . I'm reluctant to admit to trying to take on American reality because it is such a pompous thing to do and an even more pompous thing to say about oneself as a writer. One of the problems with Philip Roth's later work is that it is so pompously preoccupied with Important American Themes. Capital I, A and T. I don't even think in terms of a unitary America anyway, or a unitary contemporary reality. This is partly because my own experience of the country is so divided and splintered between the nineteenth-century Midwestern childhood I had and the ongoing nineteenth-century vestiges of a Protestant ethic that I inherited from my parents and grandparents, and the faster-moving and more jaded, sophisticated coastal world I now spend most of my time in. The primary fact about the country as I see it is that it is multi-partite and eclectic and pluralistic. It tends to make a fool of anyone who tries to write about Important American Themes.

. . . I feel that the best work contemporary writers do on America has to do with the way it sounds. Even in Germany, where I love to go because people take books so seriously, I often have to stop and say, 'Do you really *get* American irony?' Just the tone of voice that pervades pretty much all speech by Americans between the ages of 14 and 28 and much of the speech of everybody else nowadays . . . there's plenty of it in England, too, but it's always a little smartypants in England. English irony is ironic even about its own irony. American irony is sincere irony, as opposed to the truly ironic English irony. All of that, when I'm away from the country for more than a month, I begin to hunger for. I think irony is the cultural flip side of American supremacy. It's perhaps not a good thing, but it does come out of the moral sense of a person. It's a fundamentally moral response to being a citizen of the crushing, hegemonic US. Like, how can you look in the mirror with all the privilege you have and all the power that is wielded around the world to sustain that privilege?

Lynn Freed

Lynn Freed's books include six novels, a collection of stories and a collection of essays. She is the recipient of the inaugural Katherine Anne Porter Award from the American Academy of Arts and Letters, a PEN/O. Henry Award, and fellowships, grants and support from the National Endowment for the Arts and The Guggenheim Foundation, among others. Born in South Africa, she now lives in northern California.

From 'The Romance of Elsewhere', *Narrative Magazine*, September, 2010

I went off to my first (and last) writing conference because I was fairly desperate for the acquaintance of other writers. More than this, I wanted to know what it would be like to be part of the writing world. My first novel had been sold by an agent, someone sufficiently new at the game to take on a writer with only a children's story to her name. It was the sort of upbeat, feminist story, quite common in the early 1980s, when women were liberating themselves all over the place. (As it turned out, the publishers changed my title without permission and produced a paperback original that looked completely unlike its contents, a sort of coy romance, with the following printed across the chest of the beauty on the cover: 'The probing, moving novel that asks the question: How much is too much for a woman to want?')

Fortunately, the book wasn't yet published when I arrived at the conference. There, over dinner one evening, a well-known writer asked me, casually, what it was about. When I told her, her face fell. *Why?* She wanted to know.

Why on earth was I concerning myself with American middle-class marital arrangements when I had a whole world of my own to write about?

When it comes to writing, I have always found questions more useful than comments. And, really, I had no answer for her except to say that I *had* tried to write about my world, South Africa, tried and failed because, really, I'd been trying to write what everyone else was writing, subject and portent, and what had emerged was standard stuff, coming from no deeply felt or known experience of my own. More than this, I'd had no idea how to do it any other way, not until that very year, when I'd found a way into a short story, just completed. And even then I hadn't seen how close I'd come to my own subject before now, right now, when she'd asked me the question.

If, as Pasteur said, 'chance favours the prepared mind', my mind, without my even knowing it, had been preparing for her question for years. In fact, versions of it had been asked me many times before, but I had shrugged them off; I wasn't ready to find the answer. And so I'd turned to subjects that seemed more accessible – the America I knew (which, as it turns out, didn't go that deep either).

Someone once gave me what turned out to be a very good piece of advice: if you want to know what to write, ask yourself what obsesses you. Assuming one is lucky enough to *have* an obsession, there is first the question of recognizing it. Obsessions tend to live with us so naturally, there in the bloodstream, that even if we do recognize them, they can be too familiar to seem worth bringing out into the light. Whatever the case, this writer's question awoke in me an awareness of what might otherwise have taken me more years, and, if I was lucky, another book, to come to, if ever – my subject, my voice, my story. And I owe almost everything I have written since to that moment.

Alan Hollinghurst

Alan Hollinghurst was born in 1954. He has published five novels, including *The Swimming-Pool Library* (1988) and *The Line of Beauty*, which won the 2004 Man Booker Prize. His most recent novel is *The Stranger's Child* (2011).

Although I am doing it now for the sixth time, I have little idea of how to write a novel, and oddly little recollection of how I did it before. This seems to me a good thing, if also a confusing and laborious one. In most other trades a skill is learnt, brought to a necessary level of competence, and then practised more or less continually and to the same specifications, with whatever adjustments may be needed with time. In novel-writing there seems, in my case at least, to be no such mechanical reassurance. A writer of romances, or detective stories, might more easily be sustained by the machinery of a genre, but I have the worrying if worthwhile experience each time of making the thing up from scratch. In fact each novel has proved harder to write than the one before, so the lessons of experience are difficult ones: don't repeat yourself, set yourself steeper technical challenges, go deeper.

Of course I have my techniques, and then my strict routines. When I finish a book (every 5 or 6 years) I feel, as well as a sense of resolution, a kind of weary emptiness. The idea of writing another book would be nauseating to me if it weren't so remote. But before long I will be visited by the first pricklings of a new situation – an indefinable advent of images, tiny scenes, rooms. These last are always important to me – the houses, buildings, their atmospheres. I start a new notebook, and anything that occurs to me in connexion with the new project goes into it. Slowly the world of a novel takes on more density, and from the muddle of details and possibilities a narrative begins to appear. The passive intuitive gathering of materials is then matched by something more actively constructive, the deciding on a shape. So far I have written two novels that run straight through, two in three parts, and one in five. These odd numbers, and their pivotal symmetry, seem satisfying to me.

All art is a matter of selection, and thus of omission. A plan is essential, since indecision is a misery, and I never write the opening page of a novel without a clear diagram of the whole book's architecture in my head; I will have a rich sense of the content of the early parts, and of the later ones probably a vision of certain key scenes. I have only once known the end exactly before I started, but I always know what will determine it. The notebooks carry on being filled alongside the slowly progressing novel itself, and are raided for thousands of small details. This is old-fashioned work, in which a labyrinth of pencilled scribbles preserves and conveys more than a well-ordered computer file could possibly do. The steadiness of the plan enables the improvisation that is the real joy of writing a novel, the incessant discovery of what I am about to invent. Everything else is hard work.

Doris Lessing

Doris Lessing came to England from Southern Rhodesia (Zimbabwe) in 1949 and lived here until her death in 2014. She published more than 50 books, starting with _The Grass is Singing_ in 1950; the most famous, _The Golden Notebook_, celebrated its fiftieth anniversary in 2012. A Companion of Honour and a Companion of Literature, she was awarded many national and international prizes, culminating in the Nobel Prize for Literature in 2007, which she was only the 11th woman to win in its 106-year history.

Preface for the _Writers' and Artists' Yearbook_ 2003

Since I began writing seventy or so years ago everything has changed for writers. Then 'I want to be a writer' meant you were in apprenticeship to a hard craft taught by extensive reading of the best that has been written. It might take years to get your first book published. You were probably going to be poor, at least at first. There was room in this design for respect for those writers who could never command big sales, might never be known to more than a discriminating minority. Stendhal said he expected to be read and understood in a 100 years' time by the happy few. He was wrong about his prospects but his stoic stance on solitary excellence was a banner that some of us, at least in our better moments, were happy to march under. Writing was a vocation, a dedication. To write for money was to sell out – never mind about Dr Johnson. Too much socializing and celebrity must be death to integrity. This was then understood by publishers: when my first book did well, they apologized for asking me to do an interview.

Dear dead days. Now, 'I want to be a writer' usually means, 'I want the bright lights, a big advance, prizes, and the bigger the promotional tour the better'.

This is true for a good many aspiring writers. There remains, and always will, a minority who know that what makes a real writer is the solitary hard slog. There are exceptions. Honoré de Balzac thrived on society, and Victor Hugo was not averse to notice. Salman Rushdie can party all night and write the next day. But on the whole it is better for writers to shun the razzmatazz. Not much chance of that these days; the publishers see to that. Yet it is bad for a young writer to be exposed suddenly to a glare of attention. Not a few have written a good or promising first novel but then the second, written in time snatched from journalists and interviewers, might not be so good, or there might be a long wait for it. But it is no use saying what ought to be, what one might prefer: one has to work inside the limits of what is.

Until recently, asked if I always intended to be a writer, I would say no, not until my 20s. So much for lying, twisty memory: I met a woman who remembered me from school, when we were 11, sitting on our beds in the dorm, and I said I was going to be a writer. I had been writing bits of this and that always, the first when I was 7. I wrote two novels when I was seventeen, but I was too raw to match up to my ambitions. One of them was social satire, about the bright young things of Salisbury, Southern Rhodesia (I was shortly to become one of them), and the other was . . . but I have no idea. Written in a kind of trance of delight at the easy way it all poured out. I could not read a word of it back. That taught me a lesson. If you have even mildly dodgy handwriting, do not use a pen.

I am glad to say I destroyed those two early novels and much else. I went on writing when I could, even when I had two small children and no sustained work was possible. I have always had to write in short concentrated bursts, because of pressures. All this time I was saying I was going to be a writer and other people said it of me, on the strength of some cocky early stories in South African magazines. Young writers brought me their work to judge and I had not had much published myself. I look back on this with surprise. I had reached my mid-20s, always saying I was a writer – and where was the evidence? I gave up my job in a lawyer's office and began on *The Grass is Singing*. I earned my living part-time and better than in a full-time office job, doing typing for Parliament and Select Committees. I was pregnant then and had a small child, luckily an easy-going one.

I finished *The Grass is Singing*. Now what to do? This was wartime. It took 6 weeks to get letters and packages to London. No airmail then, it had to be by sea, by convoy through the submarine-haunted oceans. When you launched your precious offspring into the mails you knew it might find a watery grave. I sent *The Grass is Singing* and some short stories to publishers and magazines, notably *New Writing*. Six weeks there, the usual delays, 6 weeks back. I am reading a book now about Matteo Ricci, a traveller to China in the sixteenth century, and when he wrote a letter home to Italy he knew it would take 7 years for a reply.

Always keep a copy of what you send out. And do not believe the promises of friends, agents, impresarios when you trust them with a precious only copy. They will lose it and not know how it happened.

I got encouraging letters and began that collection of rejection slips which is essential discipline for every writer. It is not a bad thing to learn patience. The novel was rejected and by the time it had got back to me, I knew why. It was too long, three times the final length. Two-thirds was social satire, but I had been too ambitious again, I did not have the lightness of touch. I threw away two thirds, and the rest became *The Grass is Singing*. It found a Johannesburg publisher who turned out to be a crook. He would take 50 per cent of the proceeds, but he didn't publish it anyway: too politically risky.

Having at last reached London I sent short stories to Juliet O'Hea of Curtis Brown, who asked: did I have a novel? I said yes, but it was bespoke. She asked to see the contract, then said she had never seen such a shocking contract. She sent a telegram to the Johannesburg publisher threatening him with exposure, and sold the novel over the weekend to Michael Joseph. It was reprinted twice before publication, but I was green, and thought this happened to every writer. The book did well. But this success was preceded by years of writing, tearing up and rewriting. When I am asked for advice by young writers I say that what makes the difference between amateur writers and professionals is that the latter work hard, tear up, rewrite and are always ready to let something go that doesn't match up. A ruthlessness towards one's dear progeny, that's the thing.

They ask, What is your routine? How do you write? Do you use a processor, a fountain pen, a quill? Do you write in the mornings or perhaps at night? Do you . . . ? Hidden in this kind of questioning is the belief that there is some trick or secret recipe; this is because all one needs to write is a biro and an exercise book, a provisioning that gives an illusion of ease. Alas, no, the trick, the recipe, is hard work.

Andrea Levy

Andrea Levy's multi-award-winning *Small Island* was adapted into a major BBC TV drama. *The Long Song* was shortlisted for the 2010 Man Booker Prize and won the 2011 Walter Scott Prize for Historical Fiction.

HOW I WRITE

My writing routine starts with the first draft. I take my tatty old A4 ruled notebook up to my local library. I approach the stairs that lead up to the reading room (where I write) with real trepidation. If there is anyone in the library that I know, then I will engage them in a long conversation and often beg them not to go but to stay and chat longer – anything so that I don't have to start writing. But eventually I settle down in the reading room and write furiously without thinking too hard until I have completed the section that I am working on.

Then it's home for lunch and a nap. I nap every day at 1 p.m. for about half an hour. Doesn't everyone?. . . Oh.

At two o'clock I have a cup of tea with my husband. At 2:30 p.m. he tries to leave so that I can start my work, but I beg him to stay and chat some more. Eventually he escapes and I sit in front of my big computer screen to type up what I had been writing at the library. I can touch type but I am appallingly bad at it. I type away, then look at the page to find what looks like a foreign language written there. But I carry on. Once I have it all completed then I finish for that day.

I carry the pages I have just written around the house. As the evening unfolds – with dinner, some telly watching, or reading or having a bath – they accompany me. If I think of any ideas that need to be added or thought about, I scribble them down in red pen. At bedtime I place the pages by my bed. I can spend a whole night turning the light on and off so I can write down the ideas that come to me. I find that time just before sleeping so creative.

With this second draft I go straight to the computer at 2:30 p.m., after the tea and the 'No please stay and chat . . . don't go yet' etc. etc. ritual has taken place. I then work through this draft one word at a time. I think of it as ironing the words out – taking it from rough to as polished as I can make it. This draft can take a very long time, and it's so intense that I usually work no longer than a couple of hours in one day.

When that draft is done I read it to my husband. I trust that if there is anything wrong with it he will find a way to tell me. Not directly, because I would divorce him immediately, but subtly . . . somehow. If he likes it I put it in a folder and then move on to the next piece. Eventually, slowly, all those pieces build up, and after a while I have a novel.

Tim Lott

Tim Lott's first book, *The Scent of Dried Roses*, won the PEN/J. R. Ackerley Prize for Autobiography in 1996. Since then he has written five novels, including *Rumours of Hurricane* (2002), shortlisted for the Whitbread Novel Award, and most recently *Under the Same Stars* (2012). *Fearless*, his first Young Adult novel, was published in 2007. Tim Lott is a prolific travel journalist and writes a weekly column in *The Guardian* on family matters.

All writers are vain, selfish and lazy, and at the very bottom of their motives there lies a mystery. Writing a book is a horrible, exhausting struggle, like a long bout of some painful illness. One would never undertake such a thing if one were not driven on by some demon which one can neither resist nor understand . . .
George Orwell

A book is a heroic quest. It is tough and has many hazards. And you have to be tough, psychologically, to last the course. I have taught many good writers who have simply given up because of a dip in their morale after about 20–25,000 words, which is when the demands of full-length fiction really kick in and make themselves apparent.

At the end of my last book I suffered an acute depression. Other moments in my writing career have produced bouts of depression as well. Writers are often quite damaged people. Some are so damaged that they don't even know they are damaged. Furthermore, writing can put you under intense mental stress.

Apart from being damaged, most writers are also narcissists. As Martin Amis once observed, 'To accuse a writer of being egotistical is like accusing a professional boxer of being violent.' Writers are often more interested in themselves than almost anybody else. That's O.K., because being interested in themselves means that they can come to understand people in general, since they too are human beings.

Given these factors, can you get support of some kind? It's tricky. You can be supported to the extent that you are allowed by your spouse/partner to devote so many hours a day to what might be an entirely unrewarding activity, financially – 'doing nothing useful' – but that's about as far as it goes. Writers groups can be helpful. But it is in its nature a lonely life. 'Real' published writers don't attend writing groups. As John Dos Passos observed, 'Writers are like fleas, they get very little nourishment from one another'. They don't show their work around either till it's finished – so there is no feedback, there is no one to pat you on the back when it's going well, or to console you when it's going badly. You are on your own. So you have to be determined, above all.

What you are looking for above all as a writer is actually not technique or dramatic principles, so much as a way *of seeing*. Otherwise it is like knowing all the technology of a camera – like a camera buff – but not having an 'eye'. Give Annie Leibovitz a cheap disposable camera and she will 100 per cent of the time take a better photo than an amateur who has a £1,000 Nikon. Because psychologically she understands what she is looking for. It is the same with writers. The 'eye' is the all-important thing – much more important than any single technique, or all the techniques put together.

There will be times when you read back over what you have read and think to yourself, 'This is absolute hollow empty boring nonsense that no one could ever want to read five pages of, let alone a whole novel that they have to pay for.'

This experience may happen scores of times, possibly even on a daily basis.

Don't worry too much about it. Dealing with crises of confidence is a large part of the struggle of writing. 'Self-confidence,' it is said, 'is given to writers without talent as compensation.'

Glenn Patterson

Glenn Patterson's most recent novel is _The Rest Just Follows_ (Faber). His non-fiction works are _Lapsed Protestant_, and _Once Upon a Hill: Love in Troubled Times_. His first film, _Good Vibrations_ (co-written with Colin Carberry) was nominated for a BAFTA in 2014.

When she was four my younger daughter drew me a picture: a green oval, a yellow line and a black capital P, which she parsed as follows: 'That's the pea you eat, the pee you do and the P you write.'

I keep it on the notice board in my study.

The Three Ps.

In my head it has become conflated with the three Ps of writing novels: preparation, production, persistence.

Preparation is all that stuff that you absorb and arrange to ensure you are able to write: the pea you eat.

Production is the simple act of getting something down, which cannot be endlessly deferred by preparation. That is the pee you do. A voiding. No one wants, or needs, to see that. (I exclude academics here and certain members of the political classes.)

Persistence is all the strategies that you deploy to make sure that the pee you do turns finally into a P you can stand by having written: a P that someone else might actually want to read.

Remember, you are an industry of one, _sui generis_. Your raw materials are not the same as other writers' raw materials. Your 'needs' are to be indulged, yea even to the point of fetishism. Of course writing can be done with a pencil and a sheet of paper, but your writing demands only Palomino Blackwing Pearls and Clairefontaine notebooks. If you can run to them, buy them. Even if it means taking a couple of buses. Bus journeys are always time well spent. Online searches less so – more chance of your getting lost along the way – but there is at least the prospect of the postman's knock at the end of them (why still so few postwomen, by the way, even now?): signatures and padded envelopes do break up a day. Besides next time the factory will – so to speak – have been dismantled and moved to another country entirely. Here it is all green biros and spiral-bound notebooks that you can pick up for a quid from your corner shop.

Respect ritual and superstition. It is imperative that you (but perhaps only you) are at your desk – your kitchen table – sitting up in bed, or indeed cross-legged on the floor of your garden shed – at precisely 5 minutes past five on the morning of the first Monday of the month; the hat is also crucial, the odd socks or the fact that you are wearing nothing whatever in between.

As long as you write.

If there is a completed manuscript at the end of it all, then all of it worked and no one can ever convince you that changing a single element of the ritual would not have brought the whole thing down around your ears.

If you don't write, then . . . how do I break this to you, in your hat and odd socks, sitting there on your shed floor? Well, you're just a bit weird, aren't you?

Tim Pears

Born in 1956, Tim Pears grew up in Devon and left school at sixteen. He has published eight novels, including *In the Place of Fallen Leaves*, *Landed* and *In the Light of Morning*. He has taught creative writing for the Arvon Foundation, the University of Oxford, First Story and Ruskin College, among others.

Why do you write? Because you're adrift, unsafe in the flow of time. Other people appear anchored, secure, sure of themselves. You write to find your place in the world.

You soon find out: there are no rules.

There's no such thing as craft, either. You have an impulse, what John Steinbeck described as 'the aching urge of the writer to convey something he feels important to the reader'.

You make notes, do more or less research, and get going: you set off on a journey with no idea of the destination. I mean, you might have the ending (it might even be the first thing you write) but that's not exactly where you're going.

Writing a novel is a total mystery.

You choose a subject, but you can't choose a theme: this comes from the depths – of childhood, subconscious, morbid fears.

As for style, I always hear aloud inside my head what I write (or read.) Every writer does this, don't they? Each line should be euphonic – though one's sense of the music of language is personal and subjective. I hope my work is intrinsically celebratory, surely one of its functions. Written, in part, in praise. Of what? Five hundred years ago I would have said God. Now I say reality. (Others say language itself.)

I consider myself a realist, absolutely – yet am forced to admit that half the books I've written mess about with reality.

We're not professionals, that's the problem. We're all amateurs, aren't we? We write for the love (or the pain) of it. Each book is a new journey. This is why it doesn't get any easier. Why the hell should it? But it does become increasingly engrossing. You find you're involved not merely in writing a particular book, but in the process of writing.

'It is my belief,' wrote Doris Lessing, 'that talent is plentiful, and that what is lacking is staying power.' Obstinacy, stubbornness, persistence, to convey that something. (Whatever the cost? No, though it's a question worth asking. You're a citizen, a man or woman with responsibility to entities greater than your art.)

More importantly than anything, I've always aspired to the aim George Eliot described, better than I ever could, as her own: 'The only effect I ardently long to produce by my writings is that those who read them should be better able to imagine and to feel the pains and joys of those who differ from themselves in everything but the broad fact of being struggling, erring human creatures.'

Because we're all adrift, unanchored, lost in the current of time that flows through us, around us, now and forever.

Philip Pullman

Philip Pullman was born in 1946 and educated in England, Zimbabwe, Australia, Wales and Oxford. He has published nearly 20 books, of which the most famous, the trilogy *His Dark Materials,* has won many prizes, including (for *The Amber Spyglass*) the Whitbread (now Costa) Book of the Year Award – the first time in the history of that prize that it was given to a children's book. He is working on a new book, *The Book of Dust.*

SOME THOUGHTS ABOUT WRITING NOVELS

1. Don't make plans. A plan is not a map, it's a straitjacket. Your imagination needs the freedom to roam wherever it wants to go, and if you constrain it the book will suffer.

2. Always make a plan. But do so after you've written the novel. When you look at the messy repetitive careless heap of garbage that you've produced over these long months, the first impulse is despair, but don't worry about that. Look at what you've got and consider how you can shape it more powerfully, more elegantly, more effectively. It's always possible.

3. Structure is not a fundamental feature of narrative, it's superficial. You can change a great deal of the structure very late on. Don't fret and worry about the structure of your work; it's the last thing you need to fix.

4. Writing a novel has very little to do with inspiration, and a great deal to do with habit. Once you get into the habit of writing novels it's more uncomfortable not to write than to write.

5. That means writing a regular amount of text at a regular time of day.

6. The answer to 'Where do you get your ideas from?' is 'I don't know where they come from, but I know where they come *to*: they come to my desk, and if I'm not there they go away again.'

7. Take no notice of what you think the public wants. If they knew what they wanted they'd be writing it themselves.

8. Don't listen to publishers, either. All they want is a book exactly like the bestseller that X wrote last year. You have a wider vision than that.

9. Don't dawdle, but don't hurry either. No one remembers *when* a book was published.

10. The most difficult page to write is page 70. The initial excitement has worn away, and you're a very long way from the end, and you're beginning to see all the flaws and problems. Well, take no notice. You can sort them out in good time.

11. If you're completely stuck, remember the best advice any author ever gave: Raymond Chandler's 'Have a man come through the door with a gun.' You don't have to take it literally. Have something completely surprising happen, something that you weren't expecting any more than the characters were. This is where you see the value of writing without a plan.

12. 'Immature poets imitate: mature poets steal.' So said T. S. Eliot. If you try that trick with a work of fiction, and it's in copyright, the law will feel your collar. But there's an artistic obligation as well as a legal one: if you steal this plot or that setting, be sure to make a better job of it than the original, or your collar will be felt by posterity, and the sentence will be oblivion.

13. Don't listen to any advice. You're the only person who knows what your book ought to be like; listen to your book, not to anyone else.

Michèle Roberts

Michèle Roberts is an award-winning writer who has published novels, short stories, poetry and essays, and written for TV and the stage. She is Professor Emeritus in Creative Writing at the University of East Anglia.

WRITING ABOUT SEX

I've always liked writing about sex, partly because the subject can feel problematic, and writing about problems can be one of the surest ways to kick-start the imagination. Sex embodies the drive to pleasure yet that pleasure can feel difficult to express in language.

Romantic, flowery language seems vague, sentimental and dishonest. Soft-porn language objectifies, pays little or no attention to inner emotions, personal history or memory. Clinical language chops people up into collections of body parts, and can simultaneously employ odd imagery: vagina comes from the Latin for sword-sheath. The Bible tries hard: the Song of Songs in the Old Testament piles up image upon image of physical delight.

As a girl comically trying to find out about sex through books, I loved John Donne's poems, which explored desire from a male perspective. At university I discovered the medieval tradition of the female Catholic mystics who used sexual imagery to describe their passionate union with God. Heretically, they bypassed male priestly authority and went straight to the Divine Lover. Some of them got into trouble for that and got burned at the stake. Catholic doctrine taught fear and hatred of the body, particularly the female body.

Some literature/porn/erotica seems to follow that sadistic track, seems based on fear of women, hatred of women, desire to punish women. But rather than call for censorship, I want to write fiction that explores the reasons for that fear and hatred, imagines them. The imagination is a form of knowing. I understand sex through imagining sex, writing about sex, not just thinking about it from a distance. Also I want when I write about sex to be brave enough to explore my own shadow side, desires that scare me or of which I disapprove. I want to write, not to be silenced.

As a young writer, I needed to break through the taboos of my era, write about women's active sexual curiosity, lust and desire. Perhaps some of today's taboos are about writing about sex at all. Young writers often feel scared of appearing uncool. Another taboo of course concerns age. But I still enjoy sex and so I still enjoy writing about it. The imagination lets us flit between ages and genders: I can be a child of six, a man of 40 a woman of 70.

As a reader, I enjoy reading anything that reinvents what sex may mean, steers clear of obvious tropes. I enjoy writing that is funny, writing that peeps from the margins, writing that employs metaphor to re-connect body and world. I like writing that flirts, teases and satisfies me so fully that I want to come.

Western culture promises that nothing is forbidden. All our appetites, and our fears of our appetites, become turned into commodities and sold back to us. Virtual sex offers an illusion of control and of freedom. Sounds like an advert for corsets! No need for messy emotions, time-consuming conversations, the vulnerabilities induced by intimacy. That's where my new novel may begin.

Elif Shafak

Elif Shafak is Turkey's most-read woman writer and an award-winning novelist. She writes in both English and Turkish, and has published 13 books, nine of which are novels, including *The Bastard of Istanbul*, *The Forty Rules of Love* and *Honour*, and her non-fiction memoir *Black Milk*. Her books have been translated into more than 40 languages.

This is the full version of an article published in the Literary Review, April 2014, p. 1.

'When it comes to the misfortunes of nations, we must not forget the dimension of time,' Milan Kundera said. 'In a fascist dictatorial state, everyone knows that it will end one day. Everyone looks to the end of the tunnel. In the empire to the East, the tunnel is without end.' There are many tunnels in many countries, similarly gloomy and stuffy, but of varying lengths, and this makes a considerable difference, 'at least from the point of view of a human life'. Turkey, my motherland, is one endless tunnel of political uncertainty. From one year to the next there is little progress in our juvenile democracy, even though no 2 days are the same.

I come from a land where politics speaks louder than art, the state has absolute privilege over the individual and self-censorship is a routine drill in the life of every writer and journalist, though we seldom admit it. Words matter in Turkey. Stories matter. Books, although hard to get published, widely pirated and sometimes banned, nonetheless do not evaporate fast. They stay with their readers. A novel, on average, is read by three, four, sometimes up to eight people. Novels are not personal items. One does not possess them. They are to be shared. They are also to be loved or to be hated.

In lands such as ours the reception of literature is all about emotions. We either adore or condemn our writers and poets, and often, for reasons that have little to do with the quality of their writing. There is almost no middle ground. Categorical rejections are commonplace. The literary world is writer-oriented rather than writing-oriented.

Novelists, in particular, are seen as public figures in Turkey. As the youngest genre in an old country, the novel was directly adopted from Europe towards the end of the Ottoman Empire. As a result the novel was introduced as the vehicle of Westernization, modernization and later on, secularization. Early authors were a male elite with a mission 'to enlighten the masses'. They spared no effort to teach their readers through their characters and plots how much of the Eastern culture to preserve and how much of the Western culture to embrace. Every character in their novels was there to represent something larger than itself. In time, this Almighty authorship, undeterred by the writings of Roland Barthes, led way to a literary tradition of Father Novelists. In a patriarchal society constantly on the look-out for a *Baba* in politics, in sports, in school, the novelist, too, is expected to act like a Father to his readers, even if, accidentally that novelist happens to be a woman.

Every Father-novelist has his or her 'fan club', like competing football teams in a hallucinatory league. Some writers are thought to give voice to the stories of conservatives; others of Kemalists; still others, of nationalists. And those of us who do not wish to belong in any ideological camp but to be simply, and solely, an individual, end up having readers from all sides, which also means we get attacks from all sides.

The connection between an author and his/her readers is a purely emotional one. Readers who enjoy an author's oeuvre will also adopt him/ her. The writer will become part of the family. In my book signings I get to know grandmothers, great-uncles together with children, distant cousins. People rarely come to a literary event alone. They turn up with next of kin, as if this was a family reunion, and the writer, a long-lost relative now happily found. I meet readers who have quotes or images from my novels tattooed on their bodies, which makes me so uncomfortable I feel my face burn each time. Sometimes they bring me food (home-made cookies, *börek* or dolma). Sometimes they give me earrings, paintings, picture-frames and paper flowers. They send me hand-made necklaces, bracelets and rosaries from remote schools, prisons or women's shelters. There is something so beautiful in these encounters that leave me with immense gratitude in my heart. These are the times when you know that the stories you produce in your lonely cocoon travel in all directions and reach out to people you have never known before and make life-long connections.

But between affection and aversion there is a thin line. Those people who applaud you today might call you 'a betrayer' the next day. The change in the tone will have less to do with your literary work than with a comment you make in an interview or an essay. That will be enough. One critical sentence about your country will zoom you from the category of 'beloved national author' to the category of 'national traitor'. When I tweeted about the shocking increase in domestic violence in Turkey in the last decade (1,400 in 10 years), I received furious responses from some Twitter followers. 'You can criticize this in Turkish, we don't mind, just don't do it in English,' said one follower. The trouble starts when authors speak up and speak out in the international sphere. The moment an author utters criticism in 'the language of imperialism' he is labelled a betrayer. Such is the weight of ultra-nationalism that even on an issue as appalling as violence against women, a writer is expected to prefer silence to words, jingoism to truth.

In countries with perpetual tunnels, words will get you in trouble. One can be indicted for publishing a book, like the Turkish publisher of William Burroughs' *The Soft Machine*. Or for translating a novel, like the translator of Chuck Palahniuk's *Snuff*. Or for a tweet, like the composer and pianist Fazil Say, who was given a suspended 10-month prison sentence for a comment he made on Twitter.

When my novel *The Bastard of Istanbul* came out in Turkey I was sued for insulting Turkishness under Article 301. The story I wrote was about an Armenian and a Turkish family with a dark, shared history. Understandably, several of the Armenian characters in the novel disapproved of the amnesia and ignorance in Turkey regarding the deportation and massacres of 1915. Oddly, their words were plucked out of the text and used as 'evidence' by the prosecutor. My lawyer had to defend fictional characters in court.

When Hilary Mantel expressed critical remarks about royal persons and the Duchess of Cambridge, I held my breath, waiting anxiously for what would follow next. Would the author be put on trial for insulting Britishness? After all the monarchy was one of the most paramount institutions in England. What could be more British than the monarchy? But there were neither court cases nor furious protesters in front of Mantel's house spitting on or burning her photos and demanding she be sent to jail. She was criticized, sure, even lambasted by some commentators; but there was a strange apolitical quality to the entire debate.

Turkish writers, like writers from Nigeria, Egypt, Lebanon or Pakistan, do not have the luxury to be apolitical. Politics is to us what the weather is to the English. We are surrounded, gripped and repeatedly depressed by it. If we care about what is happening around us, we cannot remain immune to politics. However, can we afford to render politics our main path in life? There are moments in the lives of nations that compel their authors to make a difficult choice. Plenty of writers from the non-Western world arrive at this crossroads, eventually choosing activism over literature. As much as I respect their decision, I can't help but believe in the possibility of finding another path: having a political stance without becoming over-politicized; being active without becoming an activist; giving voice to the voiceless without belonging in any subculture or collective identity; staying anchored in fiction without cutting ties with social reality. Can we write novels that send out political echoes without directly speaking the language of politics, which is bound to be narrow and dualistic? As Camus pointed out, 'Our era forces us to take an interest in it. The writers of today know this. If they speak up, they are criticized and attacked. If they become modest and keep silent, they are vociferously blamed for their silence.'

One way or another, there is guilt. If we prioritize literature, and opt for writing about imaginary things rather than the things we hear and observe, we feel guilty for not being more outspoken, Ai Weiwei style. If we spend more time playing a public-political role, we feel guilty for neglecting our art, creativity and especially, the solitude that the craft demands.

We non-Western authors from tunnel-territories are bound to remain incomplete, fragmented individuals, emotionally split inside, juggling conflicting selves, hopping back and forth over the chasm that has opened up between our minds and our hearts. Perhaps this is what it means to be a storyteller from parts of the world where democracy is a mirage, so close, so unreachable. We vacillate between a suspicion that art and literature are in vain when civic liberties are threatened and lives are in danger, and a stubborn belief that no matter how depressing the situation, the need for stories is as urgent as ever. It is a dilemma that many authors have gone through and many more will do. But it is also worth remembering that Naguib Mahfouz's *Cairo Moderne*, Chinua Achebe's *Things Fall Apart* or Amos Oz's *A Tale of Love and Darkness* not only reveal political truths about their respective societies, but also show us that somewhere inside the tunnel burns the lamp of imagination.

Evelyn Toynton

Evelyn Toynton, an American living in Norfolk, is the author of the novels *Modern Art*, a *New York Times* Notable Book of the Year, and *The Oriental Wife*, to which Magnus Films has bought the screen rights. Her book on Jackson Pollock was published by Yale University Press in 2012. She has just completed the first of her novels to be set in England.

One of the continual surprises about writing fiction, for me at least, is how much peculiar research I find myself doing along the way. Some of the questions that arise are purely factual, and therefore relatively easy to answer: When do the tulips come into bloom in Regent's Park? What was the price of leather gloves, or butter or a first-class stamp, in America in 1937?

But others are trickier. The heroine's lover is a violinist in a second-tier chamber ensemble touring the lesser metropolises of the American midwest. Does he get his own hotel room, or does he have to share with the cellist? And – since he is living in an age before computerized music – can he supplement his income between tours by playing music for, say, deodorant ads on TV?

I once had a character who was a junkie from a relatively affluent background; assuming she still retained some middle-class sense of self-preservation, how would she get hold of clean syringes? Is it possible that heroin dealers provide them for an extra fee? And how could I find out?

In one of my novels there was a creepy leftist agitator in Ann Arbor; in another, a womanizing Russian mathematician obsessed with an alternative set theory based on mystical religious practices outlawed by the Czar. There was also a geneticist studying an unusually promiscuous species of vole. Grappling with Marxist jargon, stumbling around in Cantor's theory of transfinite numbers, investigating the sex life of rodents: who would have thought that writing a novel required such unromantic labours as that?

The hope, of course, is that the research will help make the book come alive – make it richer and truer rather than weighing it down. But quite often it proves completely useless. In later drafts my left-wing agitator was reborn as a Finnish anthropologist. The violinist became first a magazine editor and then the head of a philanthropic foundation endowed by his rich father-in-law: away with deodorant ads. After a year, the junkie morphed into a poverty lawyer with insomnia (the one subject on which I, like many other novelists I know, might be called an expert); six months later, in her final incarnation, she was a philosophy graduate student editing translations from the Khmer language. So a memoir called *Heroin from A to Z* and a monograph entitled *From Vietnam, Laos, and Cambodia: A Refugee Experience in the United States* nestle against each other on my bookshelf.

I suspect that every fiction writer has similar stories of literary meta-morphosis. But my own favourite concerns a poet. Jean Stafford always claimed that when she converted to Catholicism at the behest of her then–husband, Robert Lowell, the poem Lowell embarked on as a gift for her confirmation transmogrified into something called *To a Whore at the Brooklyn Navy Yard*. Interestingly, there is no trace of such a poem in any of Lowell's published collections. Did the whore, too, mutate into someone (or even something) else? Or did Stafford, a writer of wickedly comic fictions, simply make her up?

Jeanette Winterson

Jeanette Winterson is a novelist, poet, essayist, journalist and playwright. She supported herself with a variety of casual jobs while studying at St Catherine's College Oxford and has gone on to produce internationally acclaimed work in many forms, for both adults and children including "Oranges Are Not The Only Fruit" and "Why be Happy When You Could Be Normal?". She is currently Professor of Creative Writing at Manchester University.

Think of writing as a rope slung across space. The rope is tight-rope and trip wire. The art of balancing takes practise and courage. It is easier to fall. Writing is a commitment to walking with nothing solid under your feet. Leaping sometimes. You are making yourself up as you go along. You are making yourself stay up as you go along. Why would you do this? It isn't right for everyone. How could it be? Try not to do it. Try to do anything but. Think about the distance and the drop. The walk between dark and dark. If you want to defy gravity then write – not badly but well. Keep the tension. Develop muscle where others don't need it. Writing is not a sedentary occupation. Listen, you will soon be dead; so will we all. The question is how do you want to live? If writing answers that question then begin. If not, don't waste your life on it.

Granta's Best of Young British Novelists 2013

This is a selection of advice from half of the group of 20 selected by *Granta* as the Best of Young British Novelists of 2013. We were both part of the judging panel for this list.

Naomi Alderman

Naomi Alderman's novels include *Disobedience*, *The Lessons* and *The Liars' Gospel*. Her games include *Perplex City* and *Zombies, Run!* She's currently being mentored by Margaret Atwood.

Beginning writers, wannabe novelists, are often encouraged to 'get to know your characters'. Find out what they've got in their pockets, decide what they read at university or who their cellmate was in Broadmoor and whether they have any picturesque scars. I run exercises like this myself – they're quite fun, as a 10-minute writing assignment.

It took a conversation with the excellent novelist Peter Hobbs to point out to me, though, that this isn't really how I create characters at all. That in fact one never can know 'everything' about a character, just as we often know very little about ourselves. The process, sadly, is more mysterious than making lists of past jobs or deciding on tattoos and stretch marks and piercings. This is especially obvious when I write scripts for actors to perform – they often explain things about my characters to me, things I'd written but not understood.

So I'll give you this: don't try to know your characters. Try to meet them. Be gentle and quiet. Don't expect to understand why they do everything. Don't expect them to understand themselves. Don't force them to empty their bedside cabinet for you or pry open their diary. They might not be that kind of person.

One of the things I am proudest of: once, I sat on a hillside so still and quiet that a wild rabbit came up, sniffed a page of the book I was holding and nibbled at it with fur lips and brown teeth. Some characters are like that. They'll come if you don't frighten them off. Be patient.

Tahmima Anam

Tahmima Anam is the author of _A Golden Age_ and _The Good Muslim_. She lives in London and is a Contributing Opinion Writer for the _International New York Times_.

On a Friday afternoon in the winter of 1998, I picked up my PhD examination papers from the Anthropology department and walked back to the house I shared with five other graduate students, a pink, under-heated three storey semi-detached about a mile from the Harvard campus. Then I made a big pot of pasta puttanesca, got into my pyjamas, and disappeared for the weekend. I didn't shower or change. I just went downstairs every time I was hungry, microwaved a bowl of puttanesca, and walked back up with a hot water bottle tucked under my arm. Three days later, layering winter coat and boots over my pyjamas, I trudged through the snow, submitted my exam, and slept for 13 hours straight.

There are two lessons here. The first is, when undertaking a writing project, make sure you wear loose clothing. I could never work in a library or a café, because it would require me to get dressed, which in turn would have me relinquish my elasticated waistband, and anyway I like to sit cross-legged when I write, which is not possible in jeans, and certainly not possible in a dress. Second, make sure you know where your next meal is coming from. Unlike some people, I can't write on an empty stomach. I can't even write if the fridge is bare and I have to contemplate braving the elements to procure my lunch. So: batch cook. Stockpile treats. Freeze leftovers. Buy pyjamas in bulk. And whatever you do, don't go outside.

Ned Beauman

Ned Beauman was born in London in 1985. He is the author of three novels: *Boxer, Beetle, The Teleportation Accident* and *Glow*.

A question that I got in a lot of interviews when my first book came out was 'Most debut novels by young writers are autobiographical – why did you take on a more challenging subject?' But I'd dispute both premises of the question. First of all, if you actually did a statistical study of debut novels in bookshops, I don't think you'd find a preponderance of autobiography: people write about all kinds of things (thank goodness). Of course, it's quite possible that a tremendous number of autobiographical novels are written but only a disproportionately tiny number get published, in which case the question pretty much answers itself.

Second, I don't think it was more challenging for me to write about eugenics and boxing and Nazi memorabilia than it was for me to write about myself. Quite the opposite. Perhaps the single greatest challenge for an inexperienced writer is to sort out the difference between what is interesting and what is not interesting. If you're writing about a subject from the outside world that is objectively interesting to any inquisitive person, that's easy. If you're writing about your own thoughts and experiences, which feel interesting to you but are almost never interesting to anybody else, it's a lot harder to avoid the sort of writing that is, as Proust put it, 'so moving for the one who writes, yet so boring for the one who reads'. Pick a topic that has some intrinsic voltage, and save yourself a lot of work.

Jenni Fagan

Jenni Fagan's critically acclaimed debut novel, *The Panopticon* is published in eight languages and the film is being made by Sixteen Films. Her second novel The Sunlight Pilgrims is due out in 2015.

1. No matter what the photographer says, never lie down in the picture.
2. On first drafts everything is allowed. When you edit, get rid of your ego and be as brutal as your worst enemy; however, you must not edit the life out of

your work. This balancing act, once mastered, will lift your writing to the next level.

3. Be economical. Great writing looks effortless, but developing that authorial lightness of touch requires skill that can only be found through practice.

4. Read everything. Once you've done that, read everything else.

5. Trust your own instincts, write for the sheer love of words.

6. Style versus content is another balancing act, one needs to complement the other or there is no point. If it is all style then a reader will not invest emotionally. Write it like you mean it, put your own emotions in there to make it real. That's what makes great work stand out.

Adam Foulds

Adam Foulds is a poet and novelist from London. He has published three novels and a narrative poem and won a number of literary awards. His latest novel is _In The Wolf's Mouth_ (Jonathan Cape, 2014).

The novel is so elastic a form that it is almost no form at all. It can be whatever you need it to be.

The struggle is to find a way of writing that doesn't require you to leave anything out. No part of our thought or experience should be inadmissible. If you find yourself consciously stylizing, neatening or simplifying, then you're writing something that is less like life and more like your idea of what fiction ought to be. This is often most evident when it comes to handling characters. If your characters are less complicated than the people you actually know, if they can only talk and behave in certain approved ways and not others, then this needs to change.

The other day, I was with a friend in the National Gallery in London where two of Van Gogh's sunflower paintings are currently on display. My friend remarked on the almost childish simplicity of the way the bottoms of the vases are depicted, single curving lines of coloured paint. Above, the sunflowers are jagged with detail, fierce and fibrous and burning. They turn their leonine faces this way and that. These two things together – the full force of commitment and skill and an equally total openness and vulnerability – have something deep to say about the making of art. You need to care so much about what it is that you are seeing, what it is you have to say, that you don't care about anything else at all.

Xiaolu Guo

Xiaolu Guo is a novelist and film maker. Her works include *A Concise Chinese-English Dictionary for Lovers,* shortlisted for the Orange Prize and *I Am China.*

THE FUTURE OF FICTION, FOR YOUNG WRITERS

To construct fantastic fiction is like constructing a second reality: an imaginative reality. Writers and artists are mostly people who are not happy with limited day-to-day life. We might dream of climbing the Himalayas while buying milk or nappies from our downstairs corner shop. Or we would prefer to be on a slow boat to China in mid-ocean as Jack Kerouac dreamt, rather than struggling to get a mortgage for an over-priced small flat. I cannot believe people just live without any imagination, or without creating something from their imaginations. To be a writer or an artist is like being a young child, creating, playing, constructing and trying and trying. For all young writers and artists, I believe that if you continue your playing, constructing, dreaming, and if you keep trying then you will be on the right track to reach your goal, even though the goals you achieve will perhaps not be your final stop. We should live in the age of wonder, agelessly.

Joanna Kavenna

Joanna Kavenna writes novels, short stories, travelogues, essays and reviews. Her latest book is *Come to the Edge*, a satire. Her writing has appeared in the *New Yorker, London Review of Books*, the *New York Times* and the *New Scientist*, among other publications.

'The novel' is a strange, baggy form and the term really just means 'written stuff which is made up' and this could apply to almost anything. Critics eagerly measure the novel and manufacture rules about how novels should be written: 'show don't tell', 'never use the first person', 'always use the first person', 'write what you know', etc. This is all good fun but ultimately meaningless. Many of the conventions of the 'realist novel' are completely unrealistic in relation to real life. In real life we never, ever squat in the minds of others, listening to their innermost thoughts. Yet we do in the 'realist novel' And so on.

'There is nothing either good or bad, but thinking makes it so,' to quote a non-novelist. Who knows, ultimately, what is a 'good' or 'bad' novel? There can be no eternal, objective judgement, just fashion and taste masquerading as law. I think you have to be as honest and unfettered as possible when you write, otherwise there's no point. If you're censoring yourself all the time then ultimately no one else will care, you'll never really communicate and you'll never attain that crazy, beautiful moment, when the novel starts to fly because you have mined your unconscious, or discerned the music of the spheres or gone raving mad with the strain of trying to write your damn novel.

The novels I love are passionate, subjective and wildly idiosyncratic, and that is their strength.

Benjamin Markovits

Benjamin Markovits grew up mostly in Texas. He has published six novels, three about Byron, one about basketball and one about a high school in New York.

When I was 16 years old, my family moved to Berlin, and Granma Dot moved with us. She was a difficult woman, chatty, but also a little phony. She sometimes had a kind of Nancy Reagan tone, though in fact she was a suburban Jewish mother from Middletown, New York. When my parents got engaged, she did her best to stop the marriage – because my mother is German and a Christian. It couldn't have been easy for my mother to take her in. It wasn't easy on my father either, but his father was dead, and Dot needed somewhere to live.

Medical problems had made her more difficult with time – several strokes, and she had lost much of her vision, because of a botched eye operation.

She was losing her words, too; she complained about this a lot. 'I can't find my words.' But I was also very close to her. I used to read to her, and my dad brought in books on tape from the library, which we listened to together. *The Pumpkin Eater*. *Finnegans Wake*. I don't suppose I understood it any better than she did.

She wore heavy dark sunglasses, like a movie star, to protect what was left of her vision, and they made deep marks on her old skin. Every day, to stay fit, she used to walk around our rented house doing her exercises – swinging her arms up and down, and carrying in her hands pink jogging weights. Counting all the time, one, two, three, four, five, until she finished her set. This is what I sometimes remember, when I think about what it takes to be a writer. Doing something every day that you don't have to do, that nobody will tell you to do, and that nobody cares if you do or not. My grandmother couldn't see herself in the mirror, but she wanted to keep her figure.

Kamila Shamsie

Kamila Shamsie is the author of six novels, including *Burnt Shadows*, which was shortlisted for the Orange Prize for Fiction, and *A God in Every Stone*.

Try to avoid talking about the kind of novelist you are. Try, particularly, to avoid talking to yourself about this. For years I used to say 'I write novels about Karachi – it is the only place I want to write about or can write about.' I could speak at length about the reasons why I must write about the place in which I'd grown up, why no other kind of writing could approach the right texture or sub-text or depth. It was only through an act of self-deception (very useful in writing) that I found myself writing about Nagasaki, in my fifth novel *Burnt Shadows* (I did it by pretending to myself that really I was writing about Karachi – this may not make sense, but trust me, it happened.) It was one of the great revelations of my writing life to find that when I thought I was talking about the kind of novelist I am, I was really only talking about the kind of novelist I had been until that point – the kind of novelist I might yet be was another matter entirely. And yet it was precisely because I insisted to myself (and anyone else who cared to listen) that I could only write about one place,

I never allowed my imagination or my ambition to stray beyond that place. Now, having rid myself of the limitations of certainty, I've just finished a novel set in Peshawar, London, Brighton, the Ottoman Empire and the Western Front; it also has a two-page section set in Karachi. I think of those two pages as a wink to my own delusions.

Evie Wyld

Evie Wyld is the author of two novels, *After the Fire, A Still Small Voice* and *All the Birds, Singing*. She runs Review, a small independent bookshop in Peckham, London.

The fiction I love reading, that I try my best to write, is not neat. My favourite characters in novels are a mess of contradictions, challenging those easy categories of good and evil, right and wrong. We can't know anyone completely – even ourselves, because the brain is a vast and unknown country. And the writing I respond to most reflects that uncertainty. My interest in a character comes from those moments of slippage – when a seemingly kind person does something cruel, or when someone with a violent history is soft and quiet. It's always a good sign to have characters that surprise you in the writing of them. If anyone looks too straightforward in a novel, I try to find their other side, the light in the darkness and vice versa. That's often where I get to know them.

I was once told that writing fiction is like organizing a party: you can decide who you invite, where it takes place, what they eat and drink – but you can't tell them what to talk about, and that's the bit that makes a party.

Part 3:
Write on

Distance

by Romesh Gunesekera

By now some of you will have recognized that these three initial sections echo Joyce's famous quote from *A Portrait of the Artist as a Young Man* about the need for 'silence, exile and cunning'. For the purposes we have here I prefer the plainer trio: silence, distance and the early issues of craft.

Distance in its grand form may be exile, but essentially distance is there between the word and its meaning in every act of writing. Distance gives us words, and writing creates distance even as it brings us closer, whether we do it with ink, graphite or pixels. Language is distinct from yelps, growls and moans. The meaning of the words we use is separate from the word itself, and distant from it. They carry meaning over distance. The relationship is intimate.

For writers the question is more practical: is it better to be close to the subject you are writing about, or do you need to be away from it?

Even as you ask this question, you can probably see the answer coming.

A. There is no rule.

B. It is both: you are close and you are distant.

In one sense you are always distant. The moment you start writing, you, your focus, your gaze, your consciousness shifts to the words rather than the place you happen to be. When you transform the material into fiction you create more distance. You may take notes in situ, and although you might experiment with spontaneous writing, it is rare that your novel will be written in the midst of the action it depicts. The idea that you might write as the Impressionists painted, out in the wheat fields or by the river, or strapped to a boat in a storm, doesn't work for the writing of a novel. Not even if the scene is a dinner party. It rarely works for the painting either. You can make sketches, or notes, but the transformation takes place at some distance. The quality of that distance is what matters, but the magnitude of the distance is what we tend to notice. And the magnitude is what we all tend to emphasize.

So the writer who makes the journey from the provinces to Paris, or from Mississippi to New York or from Trinidad to London and yet writes about those earlier places seems to have used distance as a special lens. But the one who simply moves from one street to another, one part of the town to another, or even from one room to another might be using as powerful a lens, just less obviously. It might even be the case that by travelling a few thousand miles you make it a little easier to find the distance you need.

In another sense, the distance hardly changes. If the writing is mostly to do with what is in you – your thoughts, your feelings, your fears – then perhaps the subject is not Cairo, or Calcutta or Chicago but yourself, and that always remains very close. In this case, there is nothing that needs to be done. You can safely ignore the issue of distance, and get on with the writing.

That is easier said than done.

For the writing to happen, a writer needs strategies. The strategies that are important are simply strategies to trick yourself into writing. Delusions of even modest grandeur don't help, as they tend to lead to fantasies that are more enjoyable the less they are written out. So one is driven back to making small pretences that might help do the writing. There is nothing wrong with using them, if they work for you. You may find that you need several of such strategies for the same book. Here are some:

1. I need to be close to my subject. So I need to go to Portsmouth, or Beirut or wherever my story is taking place.

2. I need to be immersed in the same world that my characters are in so I can hear how they speak. So I must live and write in Santiago, or Kathmandu.

3. I need to know what it feels like to walk in among the tea bushes of Kandy, or the ice of the Arctic. So I must go there.

4. I need an objective perspective, so I must leave the scene of my story and go as far away as possible. I need a retreat.

5. I need contrast for clarity to see what I need to see. So I can only write about a village in a jungle if I am in Bloomsbury.

6. I need to be away from the real place to reflect on it: London from Bath, Cairo from London, Lagos from New York.

7. I need the place to be still, not constantly change as I look at it.

8. I need to be closer to the place in my imagination.

9. The place of my story is not a place I can go to physically.

10. It is all in my memory. What I need is to find the right trigger.

Whatever you do, and whatever your preferences, the chances are you will go through a number of stages as you settle into writing a novel.

There will be a gathering stage, which might have been all your life, or the last few years or months.

There will be a confusing stage when you don't know what the material is. Or if you do know what it is, you don't know what you want to do with it, if anything.

A third stage is often the one of false starts. Writing a novel needs more determination behind it than a New Year's resolution. It needs some organizing and getting the time right. You need to be able to give it the time it needs. So a flush of enthusiasm that lasts a week or two is not enough. The enthusiasm is necessary, but you need to be able to follow through and feed that enthusiasm with time. So there will be false starts, until you are ready to give it your all.

And then there will be a stage of experimentation. You try this way of writing, or that, you try to focus on a character or a style. The experimenting will continue but the trick is to keep going. Keep the novel growing.

The keep going stage will be one of ups and downs. One day everything will be working wonderfully well and a real story will be underway, and the next day nothing may make sense and the whole novel will seem to fall apart.

That will carry on until you reach the stage of completion.

At that point you need another kind of distance. You need to be able to step back and look at the creature you have produced and see what could be made better. Do not despair. Anything, and everything, can be made better.

Silence

by Romesh Gunesekera

The shift in human evolution from talk to writing was a shift from sound to silence. They say it happened around 3,500 years ago. I wouldn't know for sure, but the idea that someone in some Sumerian town started recording merchandise with marks on clay tablets and gave birth to writing sounds good, and like any good story, plausible. I can imagine the commotion around the merchant as he made his strange designs. He didn't need silence around him. He was probably in a bazaar. Before writing developed into pictographs, ideographs and alphabets it was simply a means of recording the conversation – an agreement – made between two people. So you might say writing was born, like most of us, making a lot of noise. Variations of that noise have continued: the thud of seals into clay, the chipping of chisels on stones, the scratching of nibs on leather, or papyrus or parchment, the racket of the typewriter, the clackety clack of the keyboard. And yet, we also know that writing needs a kind of silence. The silence that the merchant in the market would have needed in his head to work out what he needed to do to make the marks on the tablet significant. The silence we need to follow a train of thought and hear a sentence as it writes itself. The silence in which someone, like Willie in *Death of a Salesman*, can at least follow the thought in his head.

I used to think I needed nothing to write but some material to put the words on: paper, screen or onion skin. I have written in cafés, in train stations, in company, in some very noisy places. But now I realize that in all those places, what I did was create some silence for myself, much as you do when you read. If the need is there, then you are able to block everything else out. When you are writing you have to do it yourself. In reading, a good book is able to do it for you.

If you want to write a novel you need to find a way of creating that silence and stillness in your mind that allows the sentences to form that will eventually become your book. Different people will have different ways in which they find that silence. For some the environment will need to be quiet, and for others paradoxically the noise in the environment makes it easier to find a tolerable silence inside. That would be the writer who needs to write in a café. The writer who needs to hear the sound of the street. This is partly to feel real life swirling around with all its clamour, but it is also a technique of finding the silence within. You might be one for whom a silent room is too deafening to think in.

Or you might be the sort of writer for whom chatter around you is too disruptive. Where even someone sipping a cup of tea or boiling a kettle is as infuriating as someone sitting behind you on the bus bellowing into their mobile phone, or the crunch of a packet of crisps coming closer like Pac-Man wanting to bite your head off. I know writers who find their whole day ruined if they hear a chair creak next door, or if someone coughs on the street. Or if someone scrapes a gate at the top of their road. They need such absolute silence that they can only find it in a padded cell or the remote peaks of the Himalayas. It makes it tough, if that's what you need. It's a lot easier if you can manage with just that inner silence in your head, or a pair of earphones. For some it is music that provides that space.

There is also something wonderful and fruitful about unexpected silence, precious silence. This is perhaps what people who write in busy places find. An urgency to the silence. The silence you find in cities at some sleepy moment in the day, or in the dead of the night. In those moments, if you are writing, there is nothing for you in the world except your thoughts and your words. And the story they tell. The only sound that impinges will be the tick of your heart, counting the words.

I like the Sufi proverb that says, 'You have only as many words as beats in your heart, so be sure to use them well.'

To be honest, I am not sure that it is a Sufi proverb, or any sort of proverb, but I think I read it somewhere, and if I haven't, I'd like to have. So now that I have written it I can. The idea is that you may have a finite number of words you can use. I reckon it must be a few million, so one shouldn't worry too much, but even so, you could run short.

With eight books so far I guess I have used up about half a million published words. Probably another half a million unpublished have gone into the making of the published. Probably about a 100,000 of that million is pure dross. Which is about right. The 10 per cent that needs to be removed from the system. So how many have I got left? A million? Two or three million? Another half a dozen books worth? One uncharacteristically big book? Who can tell? Maybe that is why one needs to be careful.

Early on one has to write rubbish to get the dross out of the system. Small complaints about the big universe. The self and the family especially. We don't really want to read about a writer and his family. We all have our own. What we want is to read about is a character. Then if we are fascinated by the character, something about their world. The writer's family and autobiography may become fascinating later, when the writer becomes a character too, but before that we want that material transformed into something more interesting.

So the novelist, having found a bit of silence, and the right distance needs to beware of:

1. Using the first 100,000 words (which are essentially dross) to write something significant.
2. Mistaking themselves and their family as significant to anyone else.
3. Spending too many words on non-fiction, because then suddenly you may not have enough for the real novel, which may yet need a dozen drafts.

Therefore, start with play and when the time is right, get serious and choose carefully. Take care how you use your words. Be sparing, don't waste, unless you know you have some left over. Even now, I am thinking: how many do I have for this piece? This book? How many for the next novel? Are there any I can re-use? Is there a means of replenishment? A place I can refill? Perhaps there is: silence.

Apart from needing that inner silence to write, you may also need it to hear what you have written. One of the difficulties all writers have, and this is exacerbated for writers of long novels as opposed short poems, is knowing what they have written. Even with a short poem on one page, you sometimes don't see exactly what you have written. You fill in missing words, images, ideas, thoughts. Even at the level of proof reading it is difficult to see what might be missing, or misprinted. Especially when you look at it over and over again. Your mind and your eye train themselves to correct mistakes. This is virtually impossible when it comes to a novel of several hundred pages. How do you know what you have written? One way is to read it aloud. Read every word on the page. And listen to what you are reading. For that silence is helpful. Other people's silence; not your own. This is when you need to make your sound. Many writers find that some of their most cherished sentences cannot be read aloud. Partly because the writer has loved them too much and ignored their faults. Reading aloud shows up grammatical faults, airs, sometimes delusions and often nonsense. It is worth doing. But not slavishly. Sound is seductive. A good reading voice can often make up for poor writing, just as a mediocre script can be made entrancing by a star performer. So you might in reading aloud get rather more excited by your prose than you should. And most novels do need to do most of their work textually on the page, despite the growth in audio books. What works for the ear is not necessarily what works for the eye. It can be written so that it works for both equally well, but that needs work.

*

The relationship between writing and learning how to write is not straight-forward. It is not like learning to dance salsa, or the waltz, where you can learn the steps and then put it all together on the dance floor. You can't learn a set of writing steps and then sit down and write a novel. At least, I don't think so.

Writing a novel, it seems to me, is the best way you learn to write that novel. Not necessarily the next novel. To do that next one, you'll need to learn everything all over again. The first may give you some pointers, but each novel will teach you what it needs and requires from you on its own terms.

As you set about writing you will discover what helps you and what hinders you. You will soon understand what kind of conditions you need to find the silence that the book you are writing demands. At different times, the same book will have different requirements; sometimes absolute external silence, sometimes a cacophony of a market place, sometimes the voices of reaction and feedback. But at some point most writers find they need some uninterrupted time for just the book and themselves. Some time and silence in which you can think through and try to remember the whole of the narrative, the whole book and what it is you are trying to do beyond writing a novel.

My experience with most of my novels is that I need some time writing it in the midst of doing other things. The story has to work hard to assert itself into my life. Then I need a stretch of time where I can give it regular, daily attention with that internal silence it requires, even if only for half an hour at a time. If I can't have that continuity, then whenever I do go back to it I need quite a lot of reorienting time. And that then eats into the writing time. Towards the end of a draft there is always a desperate need for undivided attention. It doesn't have to stretch for weeks; it could be as little as a day, but a whole day where nothing else can even begin to compete for attention. And then I will need more time to go over the draft and make it better. Again and again. And then at some point I will need the opposite of silence. With every book I have written, I have had a draft which I have read and edited on the move. In unfamiliar places, in the midst of noise. I need to read the book the way it will be read by readers, to see if it works. Do the words still work read on a train, in the tube, on a bus or while desperate to sleep? This was how my previous books were written. But it doesn't mean that the next book will have the same requirements. I have to wait to find out.

It does help to know some things about yourself.

1. Do you need quiet to write?
2. Do you need a special place to write?
3. Have you arranged to have the time to write regularly?
4. When you have a first draft done, will you have time to read it?
5. Do you know when and where?

Early issues

by Romesh Gunesekera

Some of the crucial early issues were covered in Part 1. Here I want to survey the range of problems you might face on day one of your journey into writing a novel. Often a writer sits down at the computer ready to start and then finds that his or her head is spinning with things that yet need to be sorted out. Suddenly it seems that there are a million decisions to be made before you can put the first sentence down. It seems as though even the first word will have ramifications that are far-reaching. So you wait a moment. Then another minute. An hour passes. A day, a week, months. Nothing is clearer. You might as well have decided to be the youngest Wimbledon Champion. It looks increasingly unlikely as the days pass and you still haven't decided which racket to buy.

So let's try to work out what needs to be done and when.

Planning

Of course it is better if you have a plan. It is so much easier to start if you have a plan. Or it should be. The trouble is that it has to be the right plan. Too often you have a plan that seemed wonderful, original and exciting while you were planning it, but on day one of writing it just freezes your blood. Just looking at the working title, or the chapter headings, or even the character's name makes you tired. Rather than raring to go on with the story, you begin a series of procrastination strategies. Day One becomes Day One of rewriting the plan. That is not good.

The first thing is to accept that you will not have a perfect plan. You don't need a perfect plan. It is better to have something unfinished, something that allows for changes of mind. Back in the first century BC, Publilius Syrus knew how to judge a plan: 'It is a bad plan that admits no modification.' I like a plan you can throw away once it has served its function. And the function of this first plan is to get you started, not to stop you.

It is an important point. All the early issues we will cover in this section need decisions. But they are not irrevocable decisions. They just need to be made so that you can get on with the writing. They can be changed at any time, and whatever is written can be rewritten, provided you are prepared for the long haul.

Types of plans

1. Simple list of bullet points
2. Time line for the main character(s)
3. Diagrams: Spider diagrams, flow charts, mind maps
4. Storyboards

Try each one out and see which works for you. The one that helps you think through the story, rather than baffles you, is the one to use. The shorter, the better. Three words might be enough for you. The point is that it should free you, not constrain you.

Group exercise

Every writer, whether novice or experienced, has a way of planning their stories. Some use sheets of paper, others have computer programs, others use index cards or Post-it notes. Most people invent their own, and many of the systems have common features. One of the best ways to improve your planning is by finding out how your peers do it.

1. Ask everyone to plan a story (choose a topic or genre) in 10 minutes.
2. Pair up and explain how each one does it.
3. Seek comments/improvement.
4. Share findings with the rest of the group.

The 'W' decisions

The crucial decisions you need to make about your novel are the traditional 'W' ones:

Who are the main characters?

Where are they?

When does the story take place?

What happens in the story?

Apart from these there are two worries for the writer trying to decide how to start: which tense to use and in which person. For a fuller discussion see the Point of View (POV) section and Nuts and Bolts section, but there is a summary in the following two boxes.

All the 'W's (who, where, when, what) are important and it would help to have some sort of answer for each of them, but I would be happy to fudge some of them just to get started. For example, you might be vague about exactly where or when the story takes place. Those new to writing are particularly tempted to be vague and unspecific. There is a peculiar attraction in the universal and the abstract, and a tendency to avoid the concrete and the specific, which comes from a fear of not knowing enough about the

---

Tenses

People get worried and anxious about tenses as though the word itself has that effect. But with the exception of convoluted tenses like the past pluperfect or the present continuous past, the tense is hardly noticed by most readers.

One needs to be aware of the overall effect and then decide what suits the pace and tone of the book.

The present tense offers immediacy, urgency and a heightened state of awareness. It feels modern although it has a long heritage.

The past tense has a wider range and can be made immediate and urgent but also allows for a more leisurely and reflective journey. It tends to give a more old-fashioned feel to the text.

First, second or third person?

For most people the choice is between first and third, although recently the more in-your-face second person 'you' seems to be becoming popular.

First person has a modern feel, which comes from our era of the witness. It seems easier as you just need to get into the character, and because the character talks a lot we might believe he becomes more fleshed out. But it is a difficult act to do successfully. You can't go outside the character's experience with destroying the illusion, and the character needs to be someone in whose company the reader is willing to stay.

Third person is traditional and offers enormous flexibility. You can do anything with it. But you need to focus closely to give it the kind of intensity and veritas that we expect these days.

---

specific and a desire to be free of constraint. But the greater freedom comes from focusing on the specific.

Most important to remember is that if you have the stamina to rewrite and rethink your book, then these seemingly important decisions need only temporary answers. All you need is an answer that allows you to start. Once you start putting the sentences down within the parameters you have chosen, then you can begin to see if what you have decided makes any sense and is within your reach. Very soon you may realize that the story needs to take place somewhere else, or at some other time, or with some other characters or from a different POV. If you don't realize that soon, then you will realize it later. No matter. That is the process of writing and discovering the novel. In all of this, the novel's needs are greater than your plans.

There are deeper decisions than the 'W', which will be the real constraints within which you will write the book. These are the decisions that are more difficult to articulate: what kind of a novel do I want to write? Why am I writing it? What is essential to it? What has to be in it? What species of creature is it? Who is telling the story?

Although all the earlier answers to Who? When? Where? and What? can change, some you may decide cannot change, because the novel you want to write must explore some experience of yours, or be set in a particular place, or deal with a particular emotion or answer a particular question. If something like this is essential, you need to know. That is what you will build on and that is what you will use to test everything that you write.

Research

How much research and when should it be done is a popular question. There is no straight answer. I am inclined to say that if you enjoy research, then use it for pleasure, but limit it so that you have time to write. If you don't enjoy research, then do only what is needed for the sentence you are rewriting. If you are in the former category you are probably going to aim for novels that need more research, if you belong to the latter you would instinctively go for the kind of novel that needs less.

Research can be addictive. Some writers will deliberately choose to write novels that require the kind of research they would enjoy doing, for example, wine tasting or boutique hotels. No harm in that, if you can make it work. One of my characters had to fly a glider. I used that as an excuse to learn how to fly a glider. It helped with a couple of sentences, which luckily made it to the final version. But was the flight necessary? No, but I had always wanted to give it a try.

Michael Ondaatje said in an interview that he had never been to a desert until after *The English Patient* was being made into a movie and he had the chance to go on location. But there are other writers who have to walk the streets their characters walk. And others for whom Google Earth is enough. Before Google Earth, some writers would spend hours examining city maps, or geographical surveys to get a feel for a place. Others would go there. Some would just imagine it. You need to do what helps you write the story. After you have some of the words down, you can ask yourself questions which might indicate the amount of research you need to do.

1. Is the story credible?
2. Would a reader with first-hand knowledge of elements in the story go along with it?

3. If the story is naturalistic, are the details true enough?

4. Are there inaccuracies that disrupt the illusion?

5. Are there anachronisms that would annoy a reader?

6. Are there factual mistakes that are not deliberate?

7. Are there areas in the book you feel you should know more about?

8. Have you overloaded the story with your research?

9. Have you fudged bits of the story because you haven't bothered to find out something you should have?

10. List the faults of a novel that annoys you for its inaccuracies and sloppy research. Have you committed the same?

Tools

It is true: you can't blame the tools.

The first tool is the language. You have to learn how it works.

Then you need the instrument by which you will write. It really doesn't matter what you use as long as it works for you. Anything can be used: fountain pens, pencils, laptops, desktops, tablets, phones. . . . Some novelists have strong attachments and can only write in black ink, or on yellow paper or on particular notebooks from Scotland, others have to have an iMac and others freeze with any Mac.

For what it is worth, here are some tips:

1. Try to use something renewable and portable. If it is a special type of pen or paper you have to have, then you run the risk of supplies running out. If it is large and heavy then you have to be where the instrument is rather than have the instrument where you are.

2. Make sure you know how it works. With a pencil, that's easy. With software and hardware it is thankfully a lot easier now. In the early days of computers, if you didn't know how to work it you lost time, or all your writing.

3. I like keyboards and machines. Computers have the advantage over typewriters in terms of labour. Each edit doesn't require retyping. The disadvantage is that everything looks better than it is, and tinkering is not laborious and therefore can last forever.

4. USB sticks and the Cloud means that you don't have to have the anxiety that writers throughout history have always had: the fear of losing the manuscript. The downside is that sometimes losing the whole lot might be the best way of rewriting the novel with real freshness, urgency and emotion.

5. Software: At the end of the twentieth century when WordPerfect 5.1 came along, it was pretty good. My early books were written on it. Jonathan Franzen says somewhere on the web that he still uses it. It is clean, easy and does the job. I moved on to WordPro, which came soon after, because I had some free training on it, and in the early days you did need training to use word-processing! I still use it, although it has glitches that skid from the charming to the frustrating. Recently one of my students introduced me to Scrivener which thankfully now comes in a Windows version. I have written a book on it, and I am using it now. I like the way it can compartmentalize sections (like WordPro) but it also has session targets, running word counts and other distractions that sometimes help remind me what to do. Unlike some other writers, I quite like distractions. I feel the fiction needs to be able to hold its own against distractions. I am happy to have the Internet at my fingertips. I can now access the Oxford English Dictionary with a click, whereas in the past even the *Shorter Oxford Dictionary* kept falling out of my hands and hurting my toes. My computer hasn't learnt to alert me when emails arrive and in any case I like to check those at specific times. I don't go for Macs or gadgets that call too much attention to themselves when I want my eye to stay on the screen. The main attraction has to be in the words.

6. Resist the temptation of looking for new instruments while you are in the middle of your first draft. Finish what you are writing and then afterwards put aside the time to sort out the next bit of kit.

7. Whatever you write on, keep it and the manuscript close. You can keep a pen and a pen drive close to your heart.

Routine, time and zone

More than anything else, writing requires time. It is not easy to calculate how much time you need to write a novel, or a bunch of novels. I can understand why people would like to have an idea of how much time will be needed, so that they can decide whether they have that much time to devote to a novel, and whether it is worthwhile. Recently I have noticed people who have come for 'taster' workshops trying to make these calculations: is it worthwhile? How much should I spend on writing? Is it worth going on a course? Is it worth buying a new computer? Will I make money from writing? Will I recoup the cost?

Sadly these are not the right questions to ask. Of course there are writers and books that make money, big money. But most don't. There are increasing numbers of writers who are excellent at marketing and can spot opportunities and write to order. If you are one of them, you don't need to be reading this. You will know exactly who you are writing for, how many of them there are, how much they will spend and how often and what colour the cover of your book needs to be to get them to buy it. You will also know how long it will take you to write the book they will buy, and how many you will be able to write at 3,000 words a day and a writing life of 40 years. And if you are not hit by a bus on page ten of book 1, you will have a fruitful and successful career as a writer. Again, if you are one of these lucky writers, you don't need any advice. And your readers are unlikely to be the ones looking at a book that might be produced by anyone who might be looking at this.

The trouble with writing and numbers is that they don't tell the whole story. Take a writer who did like numbers: Hemingway. He did word counts as obsessively as he measured his weight. On the wall of his house in Havana he'd mark his weight in pencil every day before going into the next room to write. He wrote standing up, sometimes naked to feel free and unencumbered, with his typewriter on the top of a bookcase and a blank wall ten inches from his nose, or whatever. He kept away from the window that had a fantastic view of the Cuban countryside and tried not to turn around until he'd done his quota. The rumour was that he'd get 3,000 words done in a day before he went fishing. But in a publishing career that lasted 35 years, he wrote ten books (three published posthumously). At best 3 years per book, and a half a year on a boat or a bar, which if each book was 100,000 words begins to look more like 3,000 words a month. Hyperbole?

Writing is perhaps more like fishing than you might expect. Patience is rewarded, and you should never trust the talk about it.

It is worth looking at the writers you admire and seeing how much they managed to write in the time they had: E. M. Forster lived 91 years, wrote six novels, J. D. Salinger did four books in about 90 years, Chinua Achebe five novels. But then you have Muriel Spark who did more than 20 novels in

50 years or Graham Greene with over 30 books of fiction in about 60 years of writing and many others.

Where did they find the time?

Routine clearly helps, but this could be a daily routine, a weekly routine or a monthly routine. You just need to know what works for you and then stick to it. A novel does take time to write and you have to give it time. And then more time. But bear in mind Anthony Trollope's view, and he was a writer who knew all about routine and time: 'Three hours a day will produce as much as a man ought to write.' (Or woman, he should have added.)

Most writers find that a regular time, first thing in the morning or last thing at night, just makes it easier to slip into the zone where the novel is taking shape. It is not the zone of planning or calculating or researching, but a place where the novel you are dreaming up lives. For some it is a state of near-sleep and close to dreaming, which even brushing your teeth would destroy, for others it is a state of full alert that requires full battle dress. You just need to know what it is and make sure you go there often enough to get the words on the page and all the pages done.

> 'Every morning between 9 and 12 I go to my room and sit before a piece of paper. Many times I just sit for 3 hours with no ideas coming to me. But I know one thing: if an idea did come between 9 and 12, I am there ready for it.'
> Flannery O'Connor

Kerouac found it took 21 days of non-stop writing to put *On the Road* on a single 20-foot scroll (and then 7 years of editing and waiting); *The Day of the Jackal* was apparently written in 90 days, but most first drafts seem to take about a year to do. If you are just starting out, it might be sensible give yourself 18 months or 2 years to do it. What it means is that you do have to be able to spend that amount of time thinking of not much more than the novel you are writing. You need to be in touch with it pretty much every day, otherwise you will find you need to start from scratch reinventing the whole idea every time you come back to it. Then the 2 years will become 3 or 4 or 5.

This is where it seems more urgent to plan your life than your novel. It may not be so easy to move house, or get married, or get divorced or climb Machu Picchu while you are writing your novel. So find the zone you need, check out the visiting hours and go there regularly. Some people, if they have the resources, may discover they need a cleaner or a babysitter, or a valet and a personal assistant or a team of researchers to give them the time to write. Others may find anyone interfering in the fine balance of that precious writing moment an irritant that drives them out of the book and up the wall. They would need to do all those practical things themselves to feel grounded and in control, even if only of a broom, because the page goes so easily out of control. But if you can manage half a page a day, whatever you do to get there, then in a year you should have 180 pages. A quarter of a page means you will need 2 years. Enough to start rewriting with. So finish with this book that you are skimming quickly, and get started.

You will also need strategies to deal with backache, Repetitive Strain Injury, eyestrain, ennui, boredom, sleepiness, the physical and mental problems of inertia, disappointment and depression. Often combined with an illusory income. Some writers try to make a virtue of these and look for a short-term gain in a quick trade-off, or find romanticism in deterioration, others try to avoid the worst of them and keep a life.

Virginia Woolf said you need money and a room of your own to write in. Gore Vidal didn't want to chase money with his writing and bow to the whims of editors, so he decided to make money first and then write.

Although Samuel Johnson made it plain that 'no man but a blockhead ever wrote, except for money', you may prefer Kurt Vonnegut's line: 'The practice of any art . . . isn't to make a living, it's to make your soul grow.'

Whichever of these rings true for you, plan your arrangements accordingly.

Finding your voice

New writers often think that the trick is to find your voice, and then the novel will write itself. This is not quite how it works. It will take more than one book for a writer to find his or her voice, but each book needs to find its voice. That is what will keep it afloat. The voice of a novel is not the writer's voice, or the narrator's voice. It is something in the prose that allows the reader to give in and allows the book to lead the way.

As a writer there is no need to strive to find your voice. It will come with the writing. When the book achieves its full shape and finds its voice, a small part of it will become yours. That in turn will grow with the next book, and the next. In due course your voice and the voice of the individual book will merge or at least overlap. If there turns out to be only one book, the voice will belong more to the book than to you and that is as it should be.

Writing tips

by A. L. Kennedy

Starting

For some ungodly reason, some new writers decide to associate incompre-hensibility with greatness. I suspect this is because they have read Proust, say, or Beckett, or Joyce with an awareness that those authors are highly thought of. And yet they have not been able to understand Proust, or whoever, and therefore have linked wilful obscurity and genius. Please don't do this. If you decide from the outset to not mean anything you will undoubtedly achieve your aim, but no one will ever want to read you. Why should they? You have decided to waste their time. It is scary to wrestle with something half-formed and give it shape and clarity – but that's the job. If you don't want the gig, don't take it.

Do you have all your research material to hand and organized in a way that will save you time?

Do you have a space to do this, a room or a corner of your own?

Do you have time set aside to do this? This means both having a daily, or at least weekly pattern of work, and having a realistic plan for at least a year ahead.

Have you addressed any technical issues: computer access, having at least one back up drive, having a comfortable chair, a desk at a good height, enough light?

Have you accessed all the financial and practical support you can? This might mean looking for bursaries, trying for a PhD or applying for residencies or grants. This might mean establishing how you're going to work with a writer's group, a group of writers, a single key reader or a mentor.

Have you notified the people you love that you will be less accessible at certain times? Have you taken steps to make sure they still feel loved? Will they still be taken care of as they should? This might only apply to children, but some partners, or relatives can be equally dependent, if not more so.

Have you set aside space in your time-table for inspiration, rest, encouragement and thinking?

If you're working with an agent or editor already involved, are you absolutely sure of what they expect from you and when and what support they will offer in return?

Don't worry if initially you feel very tired while writing. The multi-tasking involved in writing real prose is hugely draining. It will take a while for you to develop mental stamina, especially before characters and plotlines have really taken flight.

Don't worry in general – it's a waste of time and energy. Try to just be glad you have the opportunity to do this wonderful thing.

And, should you be feeling very exhilarated by the joy of getting a run at your first novel, try to remember not to exhaust yourself or commit to crazy hours you can't sustain.

Keeping on

Remember to monitor your fatigue levels and to pace yourself in a way that means you can produce well and as easily as possible. This will vary from person to person, so you may need to experiment with whether you prosper better with long sprints, or steady trotting or a variety of approaches. This may well involve a compromise you have reached involving valuable time and space to work.

Remember to inspire yourself.

Remember to seek out others who will inspire you.

Don't hand over work to be read until you're ready to.

Try not to expose your work to too many conflicting opinions while it's in progress.

Look after your health and if you're ill – stop. The book will still be there when you're better and while you're recovering you can think.

If you get a block at around the 100/130 page mark this is no cause for panic – it usually means you have diverged too far from an inadequate initial plan, or have planned insufficiently to go forward without further consideration. Just go back to your research and also study what text you have and what it seems to be telling you about its best possible form. Then you may well undertake your first exciting and interesting major rewrite.

Try to move forward fairly fast. Nit-picking at every word can choke off your flow and is not necessarily helpful at this stage, anyway, because you will still have to rewrite.

If you're leaning on external elements – a daily hug, chats with a friend – make sure the traffic isn't all one way. Being selfish ends up being counterproductive, because you have no idea how long you're going to need help. Other elements that keep you going – even something as apparently innocent as coffee – can backfire. Doing long days on caffeine, followed by sleepless nights followed by groggy mornings propped up by more caffeine, can end up being punishing and weird. Chemicals beyond that level pretty much always take more than they give.

Don't feel the position of sections is set in stone – it may be that you have misjudged where something may best lie. Sections are quite easy to pull out and move around, both technologically and in terms of narrative. You will generally know a move was the right one when the piece settles into place as if it should always have been there.

Try to keep in mind your major themes and intentions. These don't have to stay static, but they also shouldn't just be forgotten and let slip in the effort of getting pages down.

Life is unpredictable and will intervene. You will be interrupted in mid-sentence and you may lose unexpected weeks, even months. Try not to waste time on despair, just spend what time you have on making notes, pondering areas up ahead, snatching opportunities to write when you can.

Remember there are few things better than abandoning a problem and going for a walk, taking in a movie, swimming and generally letting your subconscious solve your problem while your conscious mind is distracted. Don't get into the habit of staring at a recalcitrant page.

And remember to end work for the day, just before your idea has been exhausted, then you start the next day with something impatient for you to write it.

Reaching the end

You'll probably be tired, but equally, this is the most thrilling part of writing a novel. Hopefully, your plot has now defined a course of inevitability and gathered a critical mass. Your characters should be doing the things they must do, and the whole structure will be helping to carry itself.

If things aren't all running smoothly, then don't fret – it is always possible to take a break away from the material, reassess, perhaps do additional preparation and research, and then get back to the book.

Nothing is broken beyond fixing – it's only up to you to decide whether it's a good investment of your time to abandon ship, or to keep on bailing and hope you reach shore.

If everything is rushing along and has its own momentum, try not to let this very good situation lead you into a final pitfall. Don't allow yourself to be swept along into a hurried conclusion. Keep your head and give it the time and space it needs. A little discipline here will save you a lot of rewriting.

Rewriting and editing

For many writers it takes years of practice to get enough distance from their work to look at it dispassionately and work on it appropriately, having identified its 'ideal form', in as far as we can ever quite reach that.

For some of us, writing relatively quickly and consenting to keep up forward momentum as long as the prose is there enough for now can mean that we rewrite with something approaching a dispassionate eye.

For others, leaving the novel for a few months and then going back to it can help to make it new.

Changing format – printing pages off, changing ink colour, reading the work out loud, reading sections to an audience of one kind or another, getting input from an external reader – can all be helpful.

Using software available to you in most word-processing programmes, such as the Find function, can help you to identify the frequency with which you use certain words. You can go through sections looking at key verbs, or the overall flavour of adjectives and adverbs, to grasp a sense of what the text can offer you as a steer for its future.

Above all, remember that you are simply trying to tell something to someone you don't know and who is not physically present. Have you done that job? All the time? Every time? Have you done it with energy, passion, engagement and mutual respect?

If your reader died tomorrow, would she or he regret having spent today reading your book?

If you died tomorrow, would you have said the best and the most you could say, the words in your heart?

There is no such thing as writer's block. Unless you want there to be. There are such things as fatigue, anxiety, burn out and distracting external factors. There is such a thing as poor preparation. All these can be dealt with, one way or another.

On the page there is not a problem you can't solve – on the page you are in a world of your own creating, what kind of creator would you be, if you couldn't solve your problems. Think things through calmly – there will always be a solution and a forward course.

Nuts and bolts

by A. L. Kennedy

Grammar

There are many available grammar and style guides which will tell you about the basic functioning of the language you are going to be using. If you feel very shaky, you can even take a course to brush up. If you're writing prose fiction and are consistent and comprehensible there is an amount of room for manoeuvre – and a character may speak from a convincing lack of grammatical expertise – but it's wise to know the basics before you set out, even if you intend to abandon all known guidelines.

From our point of view, it's useful to know the general qualities of particular elements when they take their place in our prose.

Punctuation

As with grammar there are clear rules set out in any number of manuals which will tell you how to operate classically correct punctuation. You can vary this according to your own style, or that of your book, as long as you retain comprehensibility. Remember that punctuation is there to help you communicate and help your reader understand you better – it divides information into discrete packets, engineers pauses and delineates characters. It is your friend when operated sanely. If you want never to go near a semi-colon, for example, you don't have to. If you do want to attempt one, you can even use it slightly unconventionally if you use it consistently – you may just have lots of debate with your copy editor, should you get that far. You can produce perfectly reasonable and fluent prose using only full stops and commas, with maybe a dash here and there. But many of us like to have more shades of pause available to us, and the comma and semi-colon have special functions which are handy.

Tenses

Past – Often a comfortable tense, it allows flexibility because you can change gear into pluperfect for a flashback, or present for intensity. It can also be slightly/very distancing. If you were writing something with a thriller-like structure, or that needed emotional punch, you might use a gear change in combination with a linear release of information to sustain tension.

Pluperfect – This wouldn't normally be your standard narrative tense – it gets rather clunky to operate, because of all those *hads*, if not *had hads*. It allows you to go further back into the past when you have a narrative already in the past. Once you have established the transition you can generally revert to simple past tense without confusion. It's obviously the most distancing of all tenses and people can just switch off during flashbacks/digressions unless the pieces have their own narrative drive.

Present – This is the most immediate and intimate tense. It can be unwieldy if you have to handle a lot of information, but can be very effective. Although it may initially seem like an exciting departure, remember that if it's your standard delivery method it will soon simply be the voice of the book and a kind of background colour unless you add actual excitement. It's a good voice if you want identification with a character's journey through the plot, and if you want information released with a heightened sense of progressive revelation.

Future – This obviously allows you to refer to things that will happen, rather than those that have happened. As the voice of a whole narrative it might become tricky, because it could be emotionally alienating and could even seem smug. But if you want a sense of prophecy, or a kick into a slightly open ending, the future tense is very handy.

Point of view (POV)

First Person – This involves using 'I' and is the most intimate voice. It can seem claustrophobic, will lean heavily on your grasp of character and may restrict your overview in a way that doesn't help your plot. But it can be intense, astonishing, surprising and highly energetic. Watch for a tendency towards digression once you really catch the voice – people do digress, of course, but your novel should have method in its madness.

Second Person – This involves using 'you' and would be unusual in a whole novel. It can produce a kind of half-way house between the first and third person with helpful intimacy and yet a sense of distance. You are not the protagonist, you are standing beside them, or just inside them. You are being invited to participate. Some readers just plain hate being, as they would take it, cast in a part without reference to who they really are. One could argue that this type of reader must have been rubbish at playing any kind of game as a child and suggest that their perhaps sociopathic levels of narcissism will mean they are not suited to reading fiction . . . and so on. But there would be no point. They will read you in the second person and not like what they find, or they will refuse to read you and there will be nothing you can do. Other readers more used to the rhetorical use of 'you' (in, for example, the paragraph above) will simply read on.

Close Third Person – This means you will be using 'she' or 'he' and yet tinting your prose with the thoughts and feelings and other character traits of your protagonists. This is definitely the most flexible and efficient voice for prose – it lends overview, can allow for great intimacy, and yet balances that with clarity. It is subtle to read and mistakes are noticeable. If you slip between Points of View, readers will notice and jumping from head to head very often can be slightly nauseating, if not irritating. Do remember that any activity or person can be described to the degree you need from any POV – it's your job to work out how. Don't panic and jump from Jill to Jack, just because you need to show us what Jack's thinking – simply observe Jack well through Jill's eyes. Within a novel different sections or chapters can, of course, be given from different characters' points of view, although there is a limit to how many new friends a reader will want to know well.

Omniscient – This voice uses 'he' and 'she' but – as it says – has omniscient access to all areas. This can be exercised with whatever degree of focus you would like, but it can lead to quite cold and flat writing. If you use this voice, you will find your own narrative voice is probably at its most exposed – the life and warmth that will keep a reader going may have to come more than averagely from you, rather than from a sense of the characters.

Layout

Do try to format your work in the manner conventional for prose unless you have a very good reason not to. Whoever reads you wants to know you're basically a fellow professional. Just give them a novel that looks like a novel – not something that seems slapdash or a sign of psychiatric unease. Modern word-processing programs' defaults are designed for office use and they need tweaking to suit us. A 2-inch margin around your text is fine, and you should justify your prose. You should indent paragraphs for clarity, unless you want the first paragraph of a chapter or section to remain unindented. There should only be an additional line space between paragraphs if this has significance – change in time, place or protagonist. The default layout will want to give you unindented paragraphs and double spaces between, as if you were writing a business letter – you're not, you're writing a novel. Your name, the page number and the title should be on every page. You should give a title page with the novel's title, your name and a contact address, perhaps chapter listings and maybe any dedication or epigraph. Editors will print off your pages to read – if you're lucky – and they have been known to drop manuscripts. Don't give them too much trouble fitting you back together again.

Some prizes insist on a bizarre layout with non-indented paragraphs and double line breaks – I wish they wouldn't. Because the reader is used to conventional prose, this cuts every paragraph adrift from every other paragraph and makes the text read like chopped liver. And you have to add asterisks or all manner of ugly and unnecessary page clutter to indicate a major change, when if you'd had access to the page break, this wouldn't have been necessary.

Do get used to using line breaks, paragraph breaks, section breaks and chapters as features which have significance. Everything that you put on the page should have meaning and thought behind it. This isn't complicated – the longer the break, the longer the pause, or larger the shift – apply as necessary. Chapter breaks don't have to follow any rules that don't make sense to you and your book – the reader will simply experience them as pauses, or places where they break off reading for a while and (hopefully) return later.

You may wish to go beyond this with fancy fonts, varied font sizes and different colours of text. Try to do so only when it's absolutely necessary – a weak text won't get stronger because it's in AR Berkley rather than Times New Roman or Arial, or half of it is sideways – you can do imaginative things with prose layouts fairly easily these days, but make sure it's part of a legitimate whole. And colours cost more – you probably won't be allowed them if you go to print.

Writing with others

by Romesh Gunesekera

Writing novels is essentially a solitary occupation. You have to do it on your own. Most of us want to be left alone to do it. You may like to write in social spaces: in cafés, or in libraries or in bars, but only in very rare cases do novelists write while they are in conversation. For most writers the novel they are writing is special, precious and secret. Sharing, which is in such vogue in every activity, is the last thing you want to do while writing it. But at some point it needs to be shown, otherwise the novel will not blossom. It has to be read. The question is when and how.

The traditional way in which the secret novel is exposed is through a first reader. This is a privileged position bestowed by the writer on a long-suffering friend, partner, spouse or other family member. It can be the best thing or the worst for both the reader and the writer. To be the first reader is not easy. They have no manuals to guide them; they rarely have a mentor or counsellor to turn to. All they have is the vulnerable relationship they are trying to maintain against this monstrous pressure to tell you what they think of this monumental work for which you have neglected them for so many months or years. They can try to please you with compliments, but you shrug them off and say you want their true reaction; they can be truthful and say it is unreadable and then suffer your animus for years to come. Or they can try to find constructive comments to make for which you will not thank them. They cannot win whatever they say.

If you are lucky enough to have an agent or an editor, then they could be your first reader. They can couch their criticisms and comments in terms of the business, which allows unpalatable truths to be spoken. 'We need a bit more narrative momentum. For the reader, you know'. Or, 'Unless Jane does something more than sip coffee, I don't think we can persuade the marketing team. . . .' But even they have a relationship to nurture, or sever.

So perhaps the comfort of strangers might be better. How do you find them? And when?

Courses and workshops

Courses and workshops, long and short, propel you from that isolated solitary existence of a secret writer to one of no-holds-barred social interaction. Suddenly your most intimate thoughts about writing, and your carefully hidden literary ambitions, have to be exposed to a room full of people you have not chosen to be friends with and who will become confidants like you've never had before. This can be daunting, and can give rise to a whole new range of tensions. But it will also give you readers and a chance to find out whether your writing communicates in the way you hoped it would.

These encounters are not unlike novels. Whether they work for you or not depends on both the course and you. The most prestigious course with the ghosts of Pulitzer and Booker prize winners may not be the one for you. The creakiest might be just what you need. It depends on the characters in it, the atmosphere of the course or workshop, and whether you are in the mood for it. Content tends to be much the same, methods vary a bit but they all come from the same tool kit. More important is the dynamic, the pace, the tone, and that comes from the people: the tutors and the other participants. Satisfaction comes from your expectations. A lot also depends on timing.

If you are running workshops, courses or mentoring schemes, remember to set the ground rules. Be clear about what will be discussed, how feedback and criticism is given, how it should be taken, how one is expected to participate. After that, be as creative as you can. The last thing you need in a creative writing course is something that is prescribed.

Workshopping

Workshopping, which is the presentation of your writing for feedback and critiques from your fellow participants, itself is useful but has limitations. If your group is cohesive and friendly and gets on together, people are likely to be too kind and will not point out when your writing is really appalling. If the group is fractious and hostile, it will be hard to dig out anything constructive from the personal attacks masquerading as feedback. On the whole, how-ever, most workshops find a middle ground where you can get some signals as to whether your writing is working or not.

Workshops can swiftly turn into talkshops. This is fine, up to a point. But whether one is choosing one, or running one, do remember that the prime focus should be the writing. You learn more by doing than talking; so sometimes it is better to spend more of the time to write rather than to talk, even when you meet as a group. When you do talk, keep the focus firmly on the words on the page. It shows what your priorities are.

What can you do when your feedback ranges from 'I love it' to 'it makes no sense'?

It's helpful if no one 'gets it'. Then you know you need to fix something. It's even better if everyone loves it, whether they get it or not. It gives you a boost. It also helps to know if people get your jokes or cry at them. Sometimes you don't know what kind of a writer you are, serious or comic, until you get the reactions.

But on the whole one close attentive reader whose values you understand is more helpful than a cacophony of competing reactions. So one of the crucial things for the author being workshopped is to understand the points of view (POVs) (yes, that again!) of other participants. Soon you will recognize the frustrated academic, the totally gullible, the ones for whom even a shopping list is Joycean, the cynic who will never be impressed even if Joyce showed up, the pontificator who doesn't read, the vacillator who cannot make up his mind and the writer who can't get out of his own book; and this will give you a way of assessing their reactions to your masterpiece.

If you are lucky enough to be in a well-functioning workshop, you will find a group of serious readers who will look closely at the work you have produced and give you constructive criticism on the quality and effectiveness of the writing. And if you are very lucky, you will be in the mood to hear that criticism and use it.

Writing exercises

This can be the fun part of a good course. The problem with exercises is that essentially they do not count. All creative writing manuals have them, as do all Creative Writing courses. They are expected and necessary and we have included some in this book; but do not mistake them for the writing only you can do. Whether you do exercise A or exercise B three times a day, from book X or Y, makes no real difference. These are means of whiling away the time slightly more interestingly than playing pool, but playing pool may actually offer a more valuable bit of material than any exercise. But the exercise will make you feel you are in touch with your writing self, which is handy when you can't bear to be in touch with the story you are meant to be writing. These are means of tuning the piano, but the sounds they make should not be mistaken for song or composition. In fact a tune created on a badly tuned piano can be a lot better than the sound of tuning: it has the vibrancy of felt experience. That is what you need. And to get there, any exercise involving your memory, imagination and language will do. But really anyone who is running a workshop should be able to make these up. It doesn't take a lot of imagination. It's much better to invent them for yourself than to pick them from a book; but if you want ideas try some of the books in the resources section at the end of this one. My advice is, don't use them as they are, always embellish them and make them your own. If you can't do it, then maybe you shouldn't be running a workshop.

But do remember the purpose of a writing exercise:

- to bring some fun back into writing
- to ground what could be a theoretical discussion in some practical experience

Too often aspiring writers talk too much and do too little. A theoretical discussion on experimenting with POV, or editing, might be fascinating. Everyone will claim they do it. But set an exercise to change the POV in one paragraph, or edit a fifteen-word sentence down to ten words and you'll see how few have really done it. There will be a brightness in their eyes and a shortness of breath in the room. And some refreshing excitement in writing. Then you can have a stimulating discussion on whether Naipaul is right to say a sentence should not have more than twelve words, or whether a sentence that runs for 16 pages can be a real success.

Collaboration

Collaborative writing can be fun. Screenwriters do it all the time, some playwrights do it. Novelists prefer to work alone. But collaborative writing can be done, there are writing duos around. In the digital age more complicated collaborations are likely to develop.

Collaborative writing is writing in partnership (not just getting editorial help, which all published writers get at some point). An old form of collaborative writing is the chain story. This is where a number of writers agree to carry on the story sequentially, passing the manuscript on, one after the other. I did one of these back in 2002 for the literary magazine *Wasafiri*. There were five other writers, and after writing each of our sections on our own we got together to read it as one story at an event in London. Fast forward 10 years, and the next collaboration project I got involved with was to write and publish a novel in 24 hours, with 20 writers in 4 countries writing at the same time on Googledocs with inputs from anyone and everyone, using Twitter and other social media. It was done! Mad but fun. Where next is up to you, but only if you find collaborative writing has some appeal.

Mentors

Writers have found mentors right through the ages. Recently more formal schemes of mentoring have been established. The basic idea is for an aspiring writer to have a longer time involvement with an established writer to help them with their writing project. This works best if you do have a specific writing project, and have started on it and need some support and guidance in completing the draft. A good mentoring scheme will offer you a specified number of one-to-one sessions, usually of about an hour each, where you can discuss your work in detail with a more experienced published writer. The mentor you choose should be one whose writing you respect. Your own writing needs to not be in the same vein, but you need to value the source of the advice you receive.

The great advantage of a mentoring scheme over a long formal course is that you get an unparalleled level of one-to-one contact with a writer of your choice. What you do not get with mentoring is the peer group, workshops, exercises, seminars and talks – the more social aspects of a course. To explore and experiment with different aspects and forms of writing, a formal course is helpful. Some MA and PhD programmes do aim to help you produce a book; but some will find a mentoring scheme with a single focus on the writing project, with no other assessment demands, more suitable for producing a publishable book.

As always, you should choose what helps you write and avoid what hinders you.

In your development as a writer there will be a time when you need to work things out on your own; there will be times when you need only the company of books. Other times you will need to dip into something like this book, simply to get the adrenaline flowing, whether through irritation or inspiration. And then for some there will come a time to test the water with an evening workshop, a weekend course or a residential week. And at some other time you may find the structure of a longer course like a MA programme exactly what you need, and when you want one person as a touchstone you may seek a mentor, formal or informal. For many writers the commitment that comes with enrolling on a course or workshop is in itself a valuable first step. It is a statement to yourself that you value writing enough to spend both time and money on. If that helps, do it.

One note of caution though. Although every novel needs the help of someone other than its author, in its infancy it is very delicate and vulnerable. It doesn't handle talk very well. Novels are very rarely works-in-progress; they are hopes very susceptible to fading. When they do turn into more of an object, they seem to develop their own anti-tamper mechanisms. The moment you start talking about it, the thing begins to sink. So although you need someone else to help you knock it into shape, there is always a risk that they will knock it out of shape.

 'Talking about what you are trying to write is like opening the shower upstairs while trying to fill the bath downstairs. It reduces the pressure.' I have had this quote in my notebook for years, but never wrote down who said it. Now I can't find a source.

An agent's view

by Antony Harwood (Literary Agent based in Oxford, England)

If you really want to write a novel, nothing will put you off doing it, not the struggle to breathe life into characters or the challenge of sustaining a story over 70,000 words or more, not the solitude or the backache, not the daunting brilliance of the novelists you read, love and admire, not the very slim odds that you are in fact capable of writing something anyone else would feel compelled to read, not the achingly long – often endless – wait to hear back from the literary agents to whom you will send your novel, not the painful wait to hear back from the publishers to whom your agent will send your novel, not the pittance you're likely to make from all your hard work, not the cold indifference that almost certainly awaits your novel when it enters the world. We all know how hard it is and, thankfully, you and a great many other people press on regardless and write a novel.

If it turns out that you happen to have written a heart-breaking work of staggering genius, congratulations: finding yourself an agent will be plain sailing and in due course you will have contracts with publishers around the world, and accolades and royalties will be heaped upon you. Otherwise, there are some rules and tips, some do's and don'ts, some frequently asked questions and things you should know that can of course be safely ignored but might be of use along the road to publication.

If your novel is less than 60,000 words in length, it's not a novel – not from a publisher's point of view, unless it's a novel for younger readers. It may be a novella or a long short story but, whatever we call it, short fiction is next to impossible to publish.

If you don't read it, don't write it. Whatever sort of novel you write, you should know where and how it will sit in the literary and publishing landscape, what novels of a similar nature precede yours, what's been done before, what's been done well and not so well, what the trends are in your neck of the literary woods. Agents and publishers are professional readers who are generally experts in their areas of interest, so they will know just how your novel does or does not fit in. It should go without saying but it needs to be said: if you're serious about writing, you must be serious about reading. To paraphrase the late Iain Banks, imagine someone who hasn't read a crime novel, and their excitement when they come up with the idea of a novel set in an English country house where there's a house party taking place, and there are all sorts of people there, a retired colonel, a famous clairvoyant, a starlet, an angry young man and so on, and there's an unexpected snow storm and they're all trapped in the house, and then . . . there's a murder! And it turns out the murderer is . . . the butler! If for nothing else, you need to know that what you've written hasn't already been done to the point of being a joke.

Story, story, story. It's very nearly all that matters these days. What thirst there ever was for fiction in which nothing much happens seems to have been quenched. Explore your characters' inner lives, ask difficult questions of your reader, venture boldly into new territory, do whatever you want, but remember always to keep telling the story.

Agents are sent a lot of novels every week – hundreds of them. Do agents read all the novels they are sent? Of course not. Like any reader, an agent might like crime fiction but not romantic fiction, might have a penchant for thrillers and an aversion to science fiction, might like just the sort of novel you like. Or not. There's no point sending your novel to an agent who doesn't particularly like the type of novel you've written, because they won't read it. Research agents before you send off your novel. If you don't know where to start, think of some writers whose work yours might sit comfortably beside and find out who represents them – most writers have their own website where you'll find the name of their agent, or look at the Acknowledgements page in a book, where novelists often thank their agent. Google agents, go to their websites and see whom they represent.

Every agent worth their salt has too much reading to get through. Some will keep you waiting a long time for a response, some will never respond at all, a few might get back to you – for better or worse – very promptly. Sending your novel to one agent and waiting to hear from them before sending it to another agent could horribly prolong your agony, so send your novel to several suitable agents. And let them know that that's what you've done – there's no harm in introducing an element of competition, and your agent will attempt to do just the same when it comes to finding you a publisher.

Don't post your manuscript to agents, email a file to them. And keep your covering letter brief: no more than a couple of lines describing what sort of novel you've written, what it's about, plus a note of relevant information about yourself, if any. If you've done your research and can tell the agent that you think they might like your novel because it's similar in some way to the work of an author or authors they represent, tell them that. If there's nothing more to be said beyond 'Here is my novel and I hope you will read it and want to represent me', that's fine. When all is said and done, the only thing that really matters to the agent is what's written on the pages of your novel.

Now you've shaken hands with an agent who wants to represent you. Some agents will ask you to sign a letter of agreement with them. A letter of agreement with a reputable agent should do no more than clearly spell out their terms of business – the various rates of commission they will charge according to the type of deal they do on your behalf, what other deductions from your earnings they are entitled to make (bank charges, the cost of purchasing proofs and so on), how soon they'll pay you your share of monies received from publishers – and the procedures and protocols involved if either of you decide to part company. Currently, the standard commission in the industry ranges from 10 to 20 per cent; an agent is entitled to commission on your earnings from a contract they made on your behalf, for the lifetime of that contract; if either you or the agent decides to quit working together, a notice period of a few months is normally required, during which the agent is entitled to complete any business started before notice was given, and to take commission on that business. Be wary of agreeing to anything other than these simple provisions.

Agents are also editors. Neither you nor your agent wants to show your novel to a publisher when you know there are problems in it that need to be fixed before it is published – you don't want to give the publisher any reason to say anything other than 'I love it and want it.' 'I love it but I think the first few chapters are slow and I saw the twist coming from miles away' translates as 'I think the author shows promise but I'm not going to offer for this novel.' So be prepared to work closely with your agent on refining and polishing your novel until you both feel it's irresistible.

Your agent by definition works for you. You pay your agent to be in your corner, to advise and guide you as necessary, to explain and help you navigate the workings and practices of the publishing and related industries, to stand up for you and fight your fights and champion your cause, to understand your work and believe in it as you do, to chase the money you're owed and pay it to you promptly, to always have only your best interests at heart.

Know your own business. Understand the contracts you sign, take an interest in what's happening in publishing, film, television, the press and in the online world, keep reading what others are writing. The best novelists are thoroughly professional novelists.

The landscape of the British publishing industry has shifted on a tectonic scale over the last twenty years. There was never a Golden Age in publishing when it was easy to publish and make a good living from novels, and no publisher has ever been seen to jump for joy at how good business is, but the mood is particularly gloomy and anxious today. The industry faces all sorts of challenges, all of which boil down to the problem of how to sell books and make money from them. Bookselling is dominated by the supermarkets and Amazon, with Waterstones the last man standing on the High Street – remember Dillons, Books Etc, Ottakar's and Borders? This means fewer outlets for books, and the price being paid to publishers for their books being driven down by powerful market forces. And low-cost e-books have taken a substantial bite out of sales of printed books, resulting in a loss of revenue for publishers and authors. Add to that picture the rising cost of overheads and alluring economies of scale, and it's little wonder that publishers have conglomerated into ever larger groups such as Penguin Random House and Hachette UK, with a market share of nearly 50 per cent between them.

And yet, and yet. . . . People still buy and read novels as much as they ever did, and publishers still need and want to publish novels. The novelists on a publisher's list are commonly the measure of that publisher's prestige and reputation, and the publisher's fortunes – the entire industry's fortunes, come to that – frequently turn on the sales of a novel, a J. K. Rowling or Dan Brown, a George R. R. Martin or Hilary Mantel. It was ever thus. Although the industry thinks in industrial terms and agents and publishers focus on the commercial aspects of a novel during the working day, because that's what we're paid to do, we all know, everyone knows, that the true value of a novel far outweighs the price paid for it at the till or the number at the end of a royalty statement. So damn the torpedoes and keep writing novels.

A brave new world: Digital media

by Romesh Gunesekera

Writing has always used technology. Except perhaps in its infancy, as in our own, when a moving finger might have traced a line in the sand. After that it has always used some form of technology to write: the word in your head moves through your body, your fingers, a device and onto some surface. Each new development in technology has a bunch of writers working with it, taking it further. I find it exhilarating.

The advent of the personal computer made an enormous difference to writers. To my mind the two most significant effects have been in labour and in fear.

Computers and word processing changed the amount of labour you need to write well. Before computers you had to have developed your skills to the point where you could get the words right within a few drafts. With a novel each draft required considerable labour. Either you were able to hone your skills so that you hit the mark within one or two tries, or you learnt to compromise. Word processing changed all that. Rewriting a draft takes only a fraction of the physical labour it used to take. The older writer who told me 25 years ago that he couldn't face the prospect of writing another book, because the labour of typing 400 pages again and again was too much to take on, would have a different view if he was writing today.

The other change is fear. For years my greatest anxiety was losing the manuscript, or typescript, I was working on. Even early computers didn't help, as files would mysteriously vanish in computer crashes. Most of the time between writing was spent making extra copies and storing them in safe places. The horror stories of writers losing their only copy of their book in a railway station, or because their house burned down, were only too real. I've known writers to whom that has happened. My own bag of early stories was stolen at Victoria Station when I first moved to London (which only confirmed in my mind how much the city valued writing). But when pocketable disks came along, and then flash drives and now the Cloud, no one has that fear of losing anymore. The relief is unimaginable. So what does the future hold now?

An alphabetical list of questions for the digital age: Chris Meade interviewed by Romesh Gunesekera

Chris Meade is the Director of if:book UK, a think-and-do tank exploring the future of the book and a champion of digital media. From 2000 to 2007 he was Director of Booktrust, the UK reading promotion charity, and was previously the Director of the Poetry Society, where he set up the Poetry Café in Covent Garden. He is also currently on a PhD programme at Bath Spa University making digital fiction: www.nearlyology.net.

Advice: For an aspiring novelist today, getting their toolkit together, what is your advice?

We're all amplified authors now, sharing our words naturally, with friends and then a widening circle of readers via social media, blogging, self-publishing and possibly via a traditional publisher, but we don't need a publisher in the way we once did. What's vital is to seek out a community of trusted advisors to help us decide when work is 'cooked' enough to share and how best to package up and sell what we've written. I'd like to see libraries as the natural hub for such a community, but they're not that now.

Book: The physical book has been around since Moses found that tablet, but for most of us the book has meant a bunch of papers with writing on it stuck together as it has been for a few hundred years. So will it continue in that form?

Paper stuck together at the edges with glue will survive I'm sure, but for some time already it's the content stored digitally that is the core version of the work, whether it's then printed and bound or downloaded or simply read on a website. My book-loving friends once swore blind they'd never read on screen and now enthuse about their kindles and iPads, so I think more will be read that way. But those that do get printed will be beautiful, tactile, making full use of print technology.

Café: Give us some clues to the equivalent of the Poetry Café in cyberspace.

We set up the Poetry Café when I was Director of the Poetry Society and I always imagined it as a virtual space too. www.poetrysociety.org.uk is the centre of a poetry community, and the youngpoetsnetwork on Facebook is another hangout for young writers. Despite the dangers of wasting time online, it's a place where writers can meet and share ideas, as well as research.

Device: What's your favourite device for e-reading and e-writing? Why? Would our readers recognize it by the time this book comes out?

The iPad or tablet is what we've been waiting for as a pleasurable means to curl up with literary works that can include text, sound, images, video, and opportunities to write about the book too. That's where literature can spread its wings and fly up above the confines of the printed page.

I like paperbacks still, and reading on the go on my mobile too, though. Maybe next we'll be able to download novels direct to our memories so we suddenly find we 'know' *War & Peace* without needing to read it at all – but I hope not.

E-book: In America it is big, in the UK it is growing, in Japan it is phenomenal, in the rest of the world it is negligible. Like a lot of innovations in technology there is a problem that e-books lock you into a system: you have to shop in the same place. The beauty of the original design of the book was that it opened doors. So how will that be dealt with?

Did it really open so many doors? The doors of libraries and bookshops can be intimidating to many, and these used to be the only places books could be found. I worked for many years in bookshops and libraries and love them dearly, feel sad to see both dwindling, but they're closing because there are frankly better ways to make the word accessible now, and we should celebrate that – and be healthily sceptical about the commercial and social forces which control those spaces. Searching and surfing open more doors than ever.

Future: What can the Institute for the Future of the Book tell us about the future of the book?

It aims to widen definitions of what a book is, was and will be. The mission statement written by the Institute's founder Bob Stein in 2007 still puts it very well:

> For the past five hundred years, humans have used print – the book and its various page-based cousins – to move ideas across time and space. Radio, cinema and television emerged in the last century and now, with the advent of computers, we are combining media to forge new forms of expression. For now, we use the word 'book' broadly, even metaphorically, to talk about what has come before – and what might come next.

In all the fuss about e-books and apps we're failing to appreciate the web itself as an astounding and never-ending book of freely accessible information and imagination.

Google: Anything you'd like to say about Google and books?

Not naming names, but I hate secretive, greedy, tax-dodging, global corporates. Then again, it amuses me how people say, 'Wouldn't it be wonderful if . . .' and then, when it happens and we get free access to it, say, 'Isn't it terrible that . . .'

The ambition to put into the public domain all the texts which previously vanished into invisible out-of-printness takes my breath away, but the ethics of how that's done are questionable. We need to ensure that search engines are guiding us to knowledge, not signposts pointing where the advertisers want us to go.

Hardbacks: What is the e-equivalent of the hardback, which was the dream of many would-be novelists for so long?

Try looking at the work of Touchpress who make apps about the planets, the elements, and a gorgeous version of *The Wasteland*; lavish productions full of clever and appropriate interactivity.

Print on demand makes it easier than ever to make a hardback book of anything, but surely the essence of the writer's dream is to be recognized and appreciated. As Benjamin Zephaniah said in an interview with if:book: 'The important thing is to publish in people's hearts.'

I: iMac, iPhone, iPad. I had a student who wrote a wonderful story about an iChild. Is 'i' before everything, or its android equivalent, the answer to all problems?

i-doubt it.

Joyce: Margaret Atwood, in a recent interview commented, that 'James Joyce was fascinated by all forms of writing . . . He'd be on Twitter like a shot.' Do you think Ulysses *would have been even longer if he had Twitter? Or just 140 characters? Would it, and all the other forms of social media, have been a distraction or an inspiration?*

I think it can be hard to decide when you're being distracted or inspired online. Noodling about on the web often feels like time-wasting, but can lead to nuggets of information and ideas. Would Joyce tweet? #yesIsaidyesIwillYes.

Kindle: Is the Kindle the Penguin of our times, or was it?

Penguin paperbacks were probably more revolutionary in opening up access to literature to a wide public, bringing down the price of books and presenting them as affordable and acceptable items to carry around in any pocket. Then again, last Christmas I found myself sitting on the toilet at midnight downloading a book I'd just bought and thought – this really is a radically new way to buy literature!

Less: Less is More was a handy tip for writers. But with digital tools the temptation is to do more and more, as there are very few physical constraints. So is the new tip More is More?

Did authors ever enthuse about having to write novels of a certain length? I don't think so. They railed against constraints until these were removed, and then began to moan about needing them.

Isn't it preferable to let the story you want to tell define the length, shape, form and distribution method that seems most appropriate for it?

More: See above. Anything to add?

It's interesting that the web has spawned a lot of short-form writing, like Flash Fiction, whereas TV has moved towards epic narratives like *The Wire, The Killing, Breaking Bad.* It seems our attention span can be stretched or tightened any which way.

I'm currently working on a novel which includes a narrative, songs, reader contributions, collaborations and live events. MORE doesn't need to be a longer and longer story; it could involve spin-off stories for a community of readers hooked by the core text; it could be work in other media. If that makes your head ache, don't panic. The whole point is that writers and readers can choose what they want from the growing menu of possibilities.

Novel: What is the biggest challenge for the novel in the digital age?

To be novel. It depresses me how many debates around fiction have become so defensive and backward-looking – there's this horror that things might change. Novelists of all people should be looking for new ways to tell stories to best express what it is to be alive today.

Openings: The opening page of the novel has had tremendous attention in recent years. Possibly this is due to creative writing courses. It's also because of the natural tendency to use it as the selection criterion when faced with huge numbers of submissions. As a result the opening pages of most manuscripts receive 80 per cent of a writer's energy, and after that the rest of the novel tends to fade. In the digital world is this even more important? Will it all be about first impressions of the first web page, the first image? Or is it more holistic?

In the olden days readers only had the blurb on the back of the book to go on. I've heard it said that self-published Kindle authors agonize over the first few sampler pages which hook readers into buying, but they won't get repeat downloads if they don't keep hold of our attention after that. There's still a hunger for big stories – when they're worth it.

And analytics can reveal not just how many visits your work received but exactly when people got bored and went away again.

Physicality: Tell me about the physicality of digital books. One of the pleasures of the paper book is that if you love it, the touch, the feel, the smell and the look all contribute to your enjoyment and memory of it. If you don't like the book – for the words in it, the emotions in it, the smell of the paper – you can slam it down or chuck it away. Physical satisfaction either way. But you can't fling your expensive electronic device quite the same way. You can certainly have the positive feelings about it, but it is not so easy to express the negative. Is there an alternative way of expressing this physical relationship with things of the mind, other than pressing the delete button really hard?

Tapping, swiping and pulling at the screen of a tablet is a very touchy-feely experience. Touchpress, for instance, makes beautiful literary apps which are a delight to handle.

If you hated an e-book enough you could always smash your e-reader, I suppose, which would be cathartic but costly. I suggest keeping a cushion to hand which you can hurl and bash and cuddle as a means of expressing your reading experience. Maybe we could market special thumpable reading cushions and make a fortune!

Quirky: What is the quirkiest thing you have come across in digital media?

Blimey – the web is a cathedral of quirk! For a fascinating digital literary mind making projects that couldn't exist on the page, try Tim Wright http://timwright. typepad.com. His Kidmapper project involved him walking in the footsteps of Stevenson's book and reading extracts to a community of readers. The New Media Writing Prize, now 5 years old, highlights a fascinating range of experiments: www.newmediawritingprize.co.uk.

Royalties: Is there a future for royalties? And the publisher-writer relationship?

O.K., so the money is the big issue. But it's not insurmountable. At one time it was widely held that everything online was always going to be free, but now we're getting back into the habit of buying chunks of digital stuff from app stores, etc.

'The publisher-writer relationship' isn't some mystical experience, and can be a feeble one. Writers need certain kinds of advice and support and they can find this in new places now.

What bugs me is that we're all being dragged into worrying about the woes of publishers. Let's get the horse in front of the cart again: writers should concentrate on making great work for readers, and let business people find ways to generate income for us and them from the results.

Search Engines: It is hard to imagine we managed without them. Are they getting better, or worse?

I fancy making a search engine that operates like the worst small local libraries of yore: closed on Wednesdays, with a limited range of titles and a grouchy librarian looking sniffy if you asked for something she/he felt was inappropriate. I hate being told what I'd like by some algorithm, but they do seem to be getting better at it.

Text: What does this word mean to you?

How about thinking of it as a fluid thing, made of words that sometimes drip slowly, sometimes pour from us, which can be uttered, scattered, enriched and evolved, cupped in our hands, held in all manner of containers? I like the idea of the Liquid Book.

Unlibrary: You were keen on unlibraries? Tell me more about that and un-books.

We ran a pop-up Unlibrary within Hornsey Library for a year. It was a room with Wi-Fi, tables and chairs, and shelves on which users could put information about themselves and create little assemblages based on their interests, with an email or twitter address displayed so others could contact them. We ran a weekly drop-in and helped launch a philosophy learning circle and a song-writing group, which still thrive. So here was a place where local readers and writers could make themselves known, seek collaborators and meet together to think and create. Why 'un'? Because it's a library turned inside out – the people and their interests are the resource, given space to mingle as much as they wish. Out of that grew the idea of the Nearlyversity: informal tutorial groups devising their own courses using free resources from the web and meeting in cafés to discuss and help keep each other on track.

Virtual Reality: Do novels do it better than computers?

You can read a novel on a computer, but YES if you mean that there is still nothing richer than the world created by words in the brain.

But let's not get complacent about it – there's so much smug, nostalgic twaddle spoken about the power of books, as if music, film, games and multimedia can't be mind-blowing too.

Websites: Lots of questions here. What should a novelist do about a website? How? Are there websites you would recommend for information on writing, as publishing platforms, for digital media?

Yes, you need a basic website now, at least as a digital equivalent of a business card. Beyond that it's up to you to decide whether you want to publish and/or sell your work there, encourage lots of interaction with your readers or none whatsoever.

Go to www.theliteraryplatform.com and www.thewritingplatform as well as www.ifbook.co.uk for good stuff on digital writing and links to much more.

X-factor: So what is the X-factor in digital media?

The good news is that there's no Simon Cowell figure telling you if you're any good or not. The New Media Writing Prize is an annual prize for this kind of work. Bringing the inspirational sensibility of literary minds to digital formats is what if: book's work is all about.

Young: Will the young read differently, since they now learn to handle touch screens sooner and better than they learn to handle letters?

Yes. Neuroscience shows that using tablet computers changes the shape of our brains. But then neuroscience shows that everything changes the shape of our brains. Young people will discover the joy of reading, watching and making on whatever tools they come across.

Zero Sum Game: Is the link between a novel and a game similar to the link between a novel and a film? Or does the digital age offer us something different?

The great thing about digital is that we can make our own links, connections and remixes. Writers can make novelish-gamey things, poemy-drawingy-bloggy things or story-essay-songy things as they wish, and put these online where readers can find them if they're looking. This age offers us amazing opportunities to make something different. Now it's up to writers to seize the time.

The seven ages of the novelist

by Romesh Gunesekera

I remember reading somewhere that readers often go through a cycle of interests according to their age. I can't remember who made the point, and now despite the all search engines at my fingertips, I cannot find the source. So I have to reconstruct the idea.

The concept comes from the seven ages of man that Shakespeare puts into the mouth of Jacques in *As You Like It*: infancy, schoolchild, lover, soldier, the just, old age and second childhood.

How would such a person read as he or she grows older? What would interest him, or her? Possibly something along these lines or so the theory would go.

Stage 1: The child-reader starts with nursery rhymes and then is hooked on adventure. All we want in these early reading years is story, story, story.

Stage 2: When we are a little older we become fascinated by magic. Tales of wizards and improbable happenings. Still stories, but far removed from the everyday. The escape from school, even if it is into a story in another school.

Stage 3: The pendulum swings, and the need is for facts. This is soldier before lover, I think, in Shakespeare's terms. Encyclopaedias, science, or to make it wider for us, we could say true stories that give information.

Stage 4: When you are fed up with facts you want romance, or love or perhaps it is just sex. Dressed up or dressed down. This stage of puberty and adolescence perhaps lasts longer in the mind than is normally assumed and may often run right through to the last stage.

This may also be the stage when as readers we become interested in imaginary people, either like ourselves or not like ourselves.

Stage 5: From there, one might find a growing interest in ideas. Books about ideas. Philosophy beckons. Perhaps justice?

Stage 6: And then suddenly imaginary people became less interesting than real people. Biography beckons. History becomes fascinating. Personal history. And even autobiography, before the self slips away.

Stage 7: And finally a return to the early delights of nursery rhyme, before oblivion. Perhaps.

Not all readers go through this cycle, and it does not happen in neat equal segments of time to the ones who do. But as readers our interests do change: at one point it might be adventure stories, another time detective puzzles, another time epic novels, history or a fascination with Wikipedia. This might give us a clue as to how we change as writers too. But I wonder whether the writer in us has a tendency to move in reverse: starting with a love for expressing language, then a preoccupation with our own story, then later the draw of history, or ideas or sex, and only then do we get to fiction: stories about the lives of imaginary beings.

As always with talk about writing, it is worth seeing what applies to you and what applies to the writers you admire. Some writers may develop from one stage into another, but others – and crucially perhaps the ones that mean most to you – may be the ones who resist that natural development. You may prefer those who stay forever in that moment of discovering language, or the ones who hang on to that sense of adventure, or find they cannot write about anything but sex, or writers whose obsession is autobiography or stories that are constructs of facts or abstract ideas. Perhaps as an aspiring writer of novels you are beginning to see where you fit in and where you want to be. Often you have no choice. You can write whatever you like, but the writing that will work is the writing that only you can do. Working out what that is takes a lot of doing.

If you can listen to the words you have written, the sentences will tell you. It is never the intention that matters: it is the result. And however much you may want your book to be an epic, or a thriller or a literary masterpiece, it will turn out the way it needs to, according to a combination of factors we don't quite understand. All you can really do is to give it time and try to help it grow. A bit like a child.

Resources

by Romesh Gunesekera

Books

I have a couple of shelves full of books on writing which I have collected over the years. Like you I am fascinated by talk about writing, and every now and again I need a shot of it. But quite often when I open one of these books, especially the ones that tell me what exercises I need to do to get my writing in shape, my heart sinks. It is about as inspiring as being told to go to the gym for 45 minutes twice a day, or else curl up and die. The latter will happen anyway, so why procrastinate?

Sometimes they do offer good tips, often in special script. I've just opened one at random and seen a section on how to write a sizzling synopsis. It tells you exactly what to do: present tense continuous, one page for every 25 page of manuscript, courier font, etc. Very heady. It ends by exhorting you to be a master synopsis writer. I am immediately convinced, until I realize I have never written one myself. Or at least nothing more than a moody paragraph with a wildly optimistic word length which I once showed my agent, and which didn't get me anywhere. I have a feeling that it might be better to master the art of the novel to the best of one's ability, than to master the art of the synopsis. Although there may be more money in the latter.

What I have been very slow to learn is that when you need something to wake you up to writing, it's not one of these you need. What you need is much simpler: to read some very good fiction, or poetry or drama. Good writing is the most energizing and inspiring thing. So pick up *The Great Gatsby* or *Madame Bovary* or *Malgudi Days* or *Good Behaviour* or whatever lit up your imaginative life, and read. You will not be disappointed.

But for the times when you don't want that shining light, but just to wallow in talk about writing, these are a few I would pick out as pretty good.

Dorothea Brande – *Becoming a Writer* (dated perhaps but a classic).

Raymond Carver – *Fires* (does light something up).

Cyril Connolly – *Enemies of Promise* (some comfort to know).

E. M. Forster – *Aspects of the Novel* (an unbeatable source).

Stephen King – *On Writing* (fascinating and clear).

For technical stuff, these are always handy:

A good dictionary, like the *Shorter Oxford English Dictionary* (or online OED).

A thesaurus that doesn't paralyse you.

A simple straightforward style guide like *The Elements of Style* by William Strunk Jr. and E. B. White, or Henry Watson Fowler's *Modern English Usage*, that gives you quick decisions on matters of style, punctuation and clarity.

For proofreading and editing:

The Concise Oxford Dictionary

Line by Line by Claire Kehrwald Cook

UK courses

The Arvon Foundation: the leading provider in the UK of week-long residential workshops. Good writers, wonderful locations and a great experience. I whole-heartedly recommend it. For the new writer it is a way of showing commitment to yourself. Yes, you will give a whole week of your hard-earned holiday time to a writing course. But it gives you time. Not enough, but enough to appreciate how important time is for writing. For the writer who is well into his or her stride, it gives time to think.

Spread the Word: a London-based provider of short courses on all aspects of writing. If you are short of time, you could spend half a day on a workshop instead of at the supermarket.

Publishers like Bloomsbury and Faber, many literary festivals and *The Guardian* all offer workshops with well-known novelists. See who they are and what they have done. Most people pick a workshop based on time and availability, much like yoga on Thursday evenings, or a foreign language class. That is practical and fine for starters, but with writing there isn't a standard syllabus. It is a bit like a novel: a journey into the unknown. You need to trust your guide.

University courses: almost all UK universities have them now. The best known are The University of East Anglia, Goldsmiths College, Royal Holloway, Bath Spa University, Warwick University, Oxford Brookes University and St Andrews University.

Mentoring Agencies: Gold Dust (www.gold-dust.org.uk), The Literary Consultancy (TLC) (www.literaryconsultancy.co.uk) and The Writer's Project (www.thewritersproject.co.uk)

With all of these, the decision you need to make is one about finance, how much are you willing to spend (not invest, please) and what company you are looking for. Some people want their favourite writers to help them, and may find them as tutors on one of these courses; others would rather keep their idols on the bookshelf and prefer to show their work to someone less inhibiting. The choice as always is yours.

US courses

There are too many courses to list here. But the process of finding one is much the same. Start with yourself and what you need at the stage you are at.

The Bread Loaf Writers' Conference is a highly regarded example of a shorter programme.

The Iowa Writers' Workshop is a celebrated graduate level programme.

The James A. Michener Center for Writers, University of Texas at Austin

The University of Michigan at Ann Arbor

The University of Wisconsin at Madison

Florida State University

Hunter College of the City, University of New York

Eastern Washington University

Virginia Tech

On-line

For advice: www.writersandartists.co.uk

For words: www.oed.com

For software links: Literature & Latte (www.literatureandlatte.com/links.php)

For new media: www.thefutureofthebook.com

For digital storytelling: www.passwordincorrect.com

Many agents and publishers have guidance pages and advice pages. Use them for a reality check.

Workshop exercises

by Romesh Gunesekera's Ten Favourite Workshop Exercises

If you are running a workshop and are stuck for ideas, or are working with a writers' group or on your own, perhaps one of these will spark something. These are variations on writing exercises used and developed by lots of different writers as they go from workshop to workshop. We each invent our own, borrow what we can and adapt where we need to. The exercises grow and spread, but their effectiveness will depend on the enthusiasm and knowledge that the person running the workshop can bring.

I am indebted to fellow writers who have been co-tutors on Arvon courses in the UK over the last 20 years, to fellow writers at universities and in projects like First Story, and to workshop participants from all over the world for these.

There is no need to have elaborate steps in these exercises. You only need to know the basic idea; then fit it into the frame you use in your own workshop, group or practice: that is, the amount of time you give for writing, who reads aloud, how much time for discussion, and so on.

EXERCISES

1. Time

- Write a piece about a place in your past (10 min).

- Write a piece about a place now (10 min).

- Write a piece about a place in the future (10 min).

Read these pieces aloud and find the common themes that run across different writers and different times. Discuss the relationship of the writer to the past, the present and the future.

---

2. Dialogue (A)

- Eavesdrop (this can be done the day before, during a break or as an immediate task outside the room).

- Write down exactly what you heard with no descriptions.

- Write a dialogue between two people with a problem to solve, again with no description.

Discuss the power and limits of dialogue.

3. Dialogue (B)

- Find a story with no dialogue and rewrite it using only dialogue.

- Find a story rich in dialogue. Rewrite it without any dialogue at all.

Discuss the role of dialogue in fiction.

4. Description and objects

- Tell a story only by describing the contents of a bag.

- Tell a story without using adjectives.

EXERCISES

5. Show and tell

- Write a series of straightforward sentences of descriptions, for example:

  The boy was sad.
  The cook was tired.
  The soldier was frightened.
  The surgeon was angry.

- Now rewrite one of these in a way that shows what is going on.

EXERCISES

6. First pages

- Discuss and come up with criteria for what makes a good first page of a novel.

- Select a dozen first pages from famous successful books and make them anonymous.

- Ask your class to identify who or what they are and whether they meet the standards identified earlier.

- So what does that mean in terms of how a novel should start?

- Pick one you like and don't know, and continue the story.

- Compare with the real thing.

- Whose is better?

7. Character

- As a group, come up with the key facts you need to know about a character.

- Develop a set of characters collaboratively by adding date of birth, gender, name, etc. in a chain form using index cards. So each card will have facts provided by several different people.

- Use these composite unowned characters to write a story.

- How liberating is it to discover a character instead of inventing one?

8. Point of view (pov), perspective and voice

1. First lines exercise

   Write up a series of first lines on a board (5 min).

2. Case exercise

   Using two of the lines from the previous exercise as your first and your last, write a story about a crime (15 min).

   - Read aloud.

   Rewrite the story from a different POV (15 min).

   - Read aloud.

3. Discuss the effect of changing the POV.

EXERCISES

9. Rewriting

- Write a story.

- Take out all the adverbs.

- Better?

- Take out all the adjectives.

- Better or worse?

- Take out unnecessary conjunctions and prepositions.

- How much can be taken out?

- 'As to the adjective, when in doubt, strike it out.' – Mark Twain

- 'The road to hell is paved with adverbs.' – Stephen King

- 'Read over your compositions and, when you meet a passage which you think is particularly fine, strike it out.' – Samuel Johnson

Procrastination

The following exercise is something I have adapted from a suggestion I read in Andrew Cowan's book on the art of fiction. He in turn had used another source to start from.

EXERCISES

10. Procrastination analysis

1. Make a list of all the things you do before you settle down to write, for example:

   Adjusting desk/chair, cleaning screens, surfing the net for new computer/software/furniture, building furniture, reading/writing a journal, rearranging folders, choosing music, researching YouTube, checking emails, replying to immediate email/correspondence, replying to last week's/month's email/correspondence, cleaning house, eating, composing book awards acceptance speech, consuming intoxicants, exercising, sorting diary, doing social media, shopping, etc.

2. Order them into the following categories:

- limbering up exercises
- clearing the decks
- establishing necessary conditions
- useful but not essential activities
- pointless time-wasting
- acts of debilitation

3. Exchange with others in the group and see how the categories differ.

4. Ask each other why. Can behaviour change? Or is it enough to know yourself?

If you still hanker for more, and more step-by-step exercises, have a look at

Andrew Cowan: *The Art of Writing Fiction.*

John Gardner: *The Art of Fiction.*

Stephen May: *Teach Yourself Creative Writing.*

Useful distraction

- Collect quotes on writing.

- Tick those you agree with.

- Strike out those you disagree with.

For example:

'A story should have a beginning, a middle and an end . . . but not necessarily in that order.' – Jean-Luc Godard

Or 'A writer is somebody for whom writing is more difficult than it is for other people.' – Thomas Mann, *Essays of Three Decades*

Travel toolkit

by A. L. Kennedy

Ear plugs.

Eye mask.

Tea bags, coffee sachets and fixings for whatever beverage would cheer you.

A couple of plastic door wedges. If you have any doubts about a door's lock – or if there isn't a lock – these can help you feel secure. Even if it simply prevents someone's dog from bouncing on you in the morning or that person's toddler from waking you with an eyeful of yoghurt.

Small first aid kit: plasters, scissors (these can't be in carry-on luggage), antiseptic and painkillers. Melatonin works for jetlag. A laxative and an anti-diarrhoeal may be something you never need, but if you don't have them when you do. . . . Motion sickness tablets may be appropriate. Bring enough of any medication you need to take regularly to cover your trip. A good multivitamin might be an idea – you may not eat well when you travel. I always carried indigestion relief – I rarely need it, but again it's much better to have it than to lie awake all night in a hotel. Sun block and insect repellent – be aware that when, for example, New Zealanders say you should always cover up, even if you're just popping out for a few minutes, they know what they're talking about. Sunburn is painful, medically risky and humiliating if you have to do a series of events with a face like a spanked buttock. Local insect repellents usually work on local insects. And if you need condoms, bring condoms.

And remember to get all the relevant inoculations or malaria tablets before you leave. Anti-malarials have to be taken regularly and will make you feel as if you're being disembowelled if you eat them on an empty stomach, so be sure you start taking them at a sane time for changes in time zones.

Passport and a photocopy of your passport if you're going abroad.

Driving licence can be handy for identification purposes. If you want to drive abroad, check that you can legally do so, and that you have the appropriate insurance.

Water-heating elements if you're travelling in Europe and want a hot drink in your room.

Power adapters.

Chargers for anything that needs charging.

Mobile phone and contact numbers for all the people who may be able to help you as you travel.

You may want the option of buying a SIM card while abroad. If not, make sure you're not going to be killed on roaming charges.

Adequate travel insurance and the access numbers and email addresses for it.

A notebook. Why not? You're a writer.

A camera, although it's often better to look and pay attention.

Business cards – some cultures really like an exchange of business cards; and even in this desperately communicative iWorld, cards can save you the bother of tapping away at various screens, shoulder to shoulder with numberless people who want to email you about things.

A throw-away email address – so that people can contact you, but don't deluge your main inbox.

A packable dressing-gown.

A panic alarm – although check what's legal where you're going.

An itinerary that really tells you all you need to know. Do check this and get one master plan so you can pick up potential glitches. And check all tickets you've been sent – people do make mistakes surprisingly often, and you'll be the one stuck somewhere because of it.

Enough money. Always have an emergency fund – in case of an emergency.

Foil blanket. It's another thing you hope you'll never need. But it's very light to pack and it will save you from the cold.

If it would cheer you to carry pictures of loved ones, then do so. Touring is gruelling and can make you feel depressed, or as if you ought to be depressed. Likewise, if you have a favourite food that you can legally carry to your destination(s), then bring it along. I had a friend who always carried her own pillow for travelling and scented it with lavender. On long periods away, I like to use a familiar mug.

Washing powder and fabric softener, if you're going to be away for a while – in Canada, the United States, New Zealand and Australia you may well be in a hotel with a small laundrette on site; other accommodation may give you access to some kind of collegiate facilities.

Your usual toiletries and bathroom necessaries.

A range of clothes – make sure you can manage to travel in a practical way, while still having decent clothes in which you can be photographed, given dinner, let out on stage, shown to Ambassadors, etc. . . . . Check your itinerary. It took me years to work out how to deal with extremes of weather and the demands of a varied schedule. Things that don't crease and look okay after mistreatment are essential.

Copies of your work – some authors (who have cars) travel with discounted copies of their books and sell them. This seems like a huge amount of work to me and most venues with any size of audience will have a deal with a local bookshop. But the option is there. If you are going to sell books – check whose toes you'll be treading on.

A small umbrella.

A supply of music. Listening to your favourite tunes can truly ease things along when you're far from your loved ones, or marooned by a flood, and the technology is there to make this very easy now. I also travel with movies to watch if I'm away for more than a week.

A small lint-remover. The number of people with filthy cars, dog-hair-covered furniture and shedding feral cats who will render you unpalatable during tours is frankly both unbelievable and unfair.

Good, appropriate luggage. Remember that a big bag will make you want to fill it. Having two or three size options is always useful and some trips will be more rugged than others. Remember than nothing destroys bags like travelling with them – cheap gear generally lasts under a year with me, and buying it has always proved to be a false economy. Having a small bag you can use for trips out is handy, as is something moderately professional-looking and waterproof to hold your books/manuscript when you head off for your event. If you use a handbag, be sure it's secure. I travel in coats with many pockets, which I find simpler.

Several pens.

Anything else that would make you feel comfortable, happy and healthy.

References

We now live in an age when so much material is available online that I no longer have a study packed with fat reference books. Having said that, I have found that the *Shorter Oxford English Dictionary* is more useful, full and flexible than the online dictionary portals. I find that the same is true for Thesauruses, and I have my *Roget's Thesaurus* to hand, rather than using the online alternatives. I also still use my books of twentieth-century timelines and chronologies – the juxtaposition of events across cultural areas, as laid out in this kind of book, can be invaluable, although you will probably end up creating one of your own in one way or another as you work. This reliance on some paper sources may be a generational thing, and I'm prepared to believe that online provision will improve.

Even if you live outside London, British Library membership is probably worthwhile – it gives you access to information online and is a great and helpful place to visit. Getting to know your local reference library is still probably worthwhile if it's a good one, like the National Library of Scotland (NLS) in Edinburgh, or the Mitchell in Glasgow, the Bibliothèque Nationale in Paris and so forth.

Depending on the nature of your research, you may well have dealings with other great resources like the Imperial War Museum – they have a phenomenal collection and couldn't be more helpful. I have found that institutions and individuals are usually immensely supportive of writers who arrive wanting to delve into what amount to areas of common interest.

These days a good computer with a broadband connection and a decent search engine can put you in touch with archives, sites and individuals incredibly quickly. If you're not confident in this area, it's probably worthwhile either taking a course, or giving yourself over to practice and exploration at home.

Basic kit

Notebook.

Many pens. In whatever colour you like to use when writing. Red ink is handy for corrections. Blue is sometimes requested by publishers for some types of correction. You may use multiple colours to designate stages of rewriting.

Supplies of paper and toner for printing drafts.

Computer.

Access to technical support.

Appropriate software that you really know how to operate.

Memory back-up.

A reliable printer.

Charts, post-it notes or other planning materials.

Good, comfortable headphones as and when noise intrudes.

A decent source of music when musical support seems necessary – either with or without headphones.

Somewhere to keep reference materials and books.

Somewhere to put your tea/coffee/beverage choice.

A comfortable chair.

Suitable light.

A useable desk, should you work at a desk.

100 milestones of the modern novel

The origin of the novel is as much debated as any other origin, whether it is a particular language, a species like Homo sapiens, or an art form. One can recognize novel-like creatures in very distant histories and stories of myths and legends as they came into written form. Although the English novel, as we usually recognize it, is often thought to begin with *Robinson Crusoe*, the European novel which still feeds the modern form began with *Don Quixote* more than a hundred years earlier. Forerunners to these are the Sumerian *Epic of Gilgamesh* (1400–1000 BC), the Indian epics *Ramayana* and *Mahabharata*, Homer's *Iliad* and *Odyssey* and Virgil's *Aeneid*; also *The Tale of Genji* (1010) from Japan, Chaucer's *Canterbury Tales* and medieval romances. The novel in its modern form draws from all these sources and more, crossing languages and traditions across the world. All novelists have these influences, whether they are conscious of them or not. The influence comes from the language itself, as well as the books we have read and the ones we have only heard about.

We have listed 100 novels from *Don Quixote* onwards that have been influential and important for other novelists. We have tried to pick only one title per author so that we can offer a range. This is not a list of books that you must read before starting your own, but it might be useful at some point to know that they exist for the light that they may shine. These are books that have changed the way novels have been written and read.

1532	*Pantagruel* by François Rabelais
1610	*Don Quixote* by Miguel de Cervantes
1657	*L'Autre Monde* by Cyrano de Bergerac
1688	*Oroonoko* by Aphra Behn

1719	*Robinson Crusoe* by Daniel Defoe
1740	*Pamela* by Samuel Richardson
1759	*Tristram Shandy* by Laurence Sterne
1813	*Pride and Prejudice* by Jane Austen
1818	*Frankenstein* by Mary Shelley
1833	*Eugénie Grandet* by Honoré de Balzac
1839	*The Charterhouse of Parma* by Stendhal
1845	*The Count of Monte Cristo* by Alexandre Dumas
1847	*Wuthering Heights* by Emily Brontë
1847	*Jane Eyre* by Charlotte Brontë
1848	*Vanity Fair* by William Makepeace Thackeray
1851	*Moby Dick* by Herman Melville
1856	*Madame Bovary* by Gustave Flaubert
1861	*Great Expectations* by Charles Dickens
1866	*Crime and Punishment* by Fyodor Dostoevsky
1867	*Thérèse Raquin* by Émile Zola
1868	*The Moonstone* by Wilkie Collins
1868	*Little Women* by Louisa May Alcott
1871	*Middlemarch* by George Eliot
1877	*Anna Karenina* by Leo Tolstoy
1884	*Huckleberry Finn* by Mark Twain
1886	*The Mayor of Casterbridge* by Thomas Hardy
1886	*Strange Case of Dr Jekyll and Mr Hyde* by Robert Louis Stevenson
1895	*The Time Machine* by H. G. Wells
1924–28	*Parade's End* by Ford Madox Ford
1900	*Lord Jim* by Joseph Conrad
1906	*The Jungle* by Upton Sinclair
1907	*The Portrait of a Lady* by Henry James
1910	*The Getting of Wisdom* by Henry Handel Richardson
1913	*Sons and Lovers* by D. H. Lawrence
1922	*Ulysses* by James Joyce
1924	*A Passage to India* by E. M. Forster

1925	*The Great Gatsby* by F. Scott Fitzgerald
1925	*The Trial* by Franz Kafka
1926	*The Sun Also Rises* by Ernest Hemingway
1927	*To the Lighthouse* by Virginia Woolf
1927	*In Search of Lost Time* by Marcel Proust
1929	*The Sound and the Fury* by William Faulkner
1930	*The Maltese Falcon* by Dashiell Hammett
1932	*Brave New World* by Aldous Huxley
1932	*Radetzkymarsch* by Joseph Roth
1934	*Novel With Cocaine* by M. Ageyev
1935	*Swami and Friends* by R. K. Narayan
1936	*Mephisto* by Klaus Mann
1938	*Scoop* by Evelyn Waugh
1938	*Murphy* by Samuel Beckett
1938	*U.S.A.* by John Dos Passos
1939	*The Grapes of Wrath* by John Steinbeck
1939	*The Big Sleep* by Raymond Chandler
1947	*The Plague* by Albert Camus
1948	*The Quiet American* by Graham Greene
1949	*Nineteen Eighty-four* by George Orwell
1950	*The Grass is Singing* by Doris Lessing
1951	*The Catcher in the Rye* by J. D. Salinger
1953	*Fahrenheit 451* by Ray Bradbury
1954	*Lord of the Flies* by William Golding
1955	*The Lord of the Rings* by J. R. R. Tolkien
1955	*Lolita* by Vladimir Nabokov
1957	*On the Road* by Jack Kerouac
1957	*Voss* by Patrick White
1958	*Things Fall Apart* by Chinua Achebe
1958	*The Leopard* by Giuseppe Tomasi di Lampedusa
1959	*Naked Lunch* by William S. Burroughs
1959	*The Tin Drum* by Günter Grass

1960	*To Kill a Mockingbird* by Harper Lee
1961	*A House for Mr Biswas* by V. S. Naipaul
1961	*Catch-22* by Joseph Heller
1961	*The Prime of Miss Jean Brodie* by Muriel Spark
1961	*The Moviegoer* by Walker Percy
1962	*The Drowned World* by J. G. Ballard
1962	*A Day In The Life Of Ivan Denisovich* by Aleksandr Solzhenitsyn
1963	*The Group* by Mary McCarthy
1964	*Herzog* by Saul Bellow
1964	*The Spy Who Came in from the Cold* by John le Carré
1965	*Closely Watched Trains* by Bohumil Hrabal
1966	*Wide Sargasso Sea* by Jean Rhys
1967	*One Hundred Years of Solitude* by Gabriel Garcia Márquez
1969	*Portnoy's Complaint* by Philip Roth
1969	*The Unfortunates* by B. S. Johnson
1970	*Bomber* by Len Deighton
1972	*G* by John Berger
1973	*Gravity's Rainbow* by Thomas Pynchon
1979	*The Book of Laughter and Forgetting* by Milan Kundera
1979	*If on a Winter's Night a Traveller* by Italo Calvino
1981	*Midnight's Children* by Salman Rushdie
1981	*Lanark* by Alasdair Gray
1982	*If Not Now, When?* by Primo Levi
1984	*An Invincible Memory* by João Ubaldo Ribeiro
1987	*Norwegian Wood* by Haruki Murakami
1987	*Beloved* by Toni Morrison
1988	*Natural History* by Juan Perucho
1989	*The Melancholy of Resistance* by László Krasznahorkai
1991	*American Psycho* by Bret Easton Ellis
1993	*Trainspotting* by Irvine Welsh
1993	*A Suitable Boy* by Vikram Seth
2001	*Austerlitz* by W. G. Sebald

End piece

by Romesh Gunesekera

> **"** *There are three rules for writing a novel.*
> *Unfortunately, no one knows what they are.* **"**
> W. Somerset Maugham

There are no short cuts. The best way to learn how to write a novel is to write one. You will soon see your weaknesses and your strengths. But to do it, you must not let anything stop you. Others have done it faced with war, tragedy and grief. You have no excuses.

There are things you can do to help you write one. As many of the contributors to this book have said, in one way or another, you need to get organized to write a novel. Sometimes you need to trick yourself into doing it.

The novel you write will be your novel. Only you can make it happen, and the result will always be the result of your decisions, not somebody else's.

Despite Somerset Maugham's quote, every writer can come up with ten rules for writing a novel. You should make your own. Here are my ten for today:

1. Expect to rewrite. As you can make it better later, get something going now.
2. Fix a time and a place for writing and stick to it.
3. Don't look back until you've got some mileage done.
4. Time is a good editor. Let time work on your writing before you do your next revision.
5. Resist the unnecessary.
6. Identify some milestones on the road and makes sure you reach them.
7. Don't try to solve all the problems you anticipate before you start, but do work out the people, the place and the period that you need for the first few pages.
8. Build up steam.
9. At some point, you have to give it your all, but don't expect anyone to notice.
10. Find the excitement on the page and believe in the magic of words.

Conclusion

by A. L. Kennedy

As I've been writing pieces for this book, I have also been in the final stages of preparation for a novel of my own, and then in the earliest stages of its actual execution. So, while trying to formulate practical help and encouragement for other writers, I have also been faced with the little turns and surprises, the unexpected joys, the knots and tangles of a real novel, developing in real time. No guide book will ever be as messy, as lovely, as infuriating, or as exciting as truly beginning to test theories, take risks, push your abilities and find your strengths while you write your own novel. I hope this book will enable you to find your own way and develop a working process that suits you and the project you are pursuing. Although it's sometimes tempting to take more and more advice, pause to read another book on writing, attend another workshop, or seminar . . . the person who will teach you how to do this, inspire you and lead you through is you. This is, of course, a great responsibility, but it's also hugely liberating and fun.

Having been away from extended prose for some time, I had forgotten just how much pure, deep fun it is to sit in front of a keyboard and be with people who interest me, who have things to do and places to visit, and who will meet each other and move beyond what I could expect for them – if I will only help them. Turning a sentence until it seems right, away from a short deadline, away from anyone else's agenda, away from anything other than the demands of a plot and characters I am anxious to express – that's immensely satisfying. I have been doing this for more than 30 years, for the whole of my adult life, and it stays new, it stays interesting, it stays educational and generous. To wake in the morning and find this is my profession – even if it no longer earns me a living – is a daily joy.

So, if I could give some last advice, it would be to take your own joy seriously, strengthen and increase it, make it eloquent so that it can be increased further in others. We inhabit an age within which short-term goals and shoddy work are allowed to pass and even encouraged. We are pressured to lower our expectations of ourselves and others, to devalue what is human and to abandon our dreams. The novel is not about that. The novel is about lasting beyond any given lifespan, it is about high levels of craft, about humanity, true intimacy and all the possibilities of unleashed dreaming. Treasure your chance to be with your novel while you can, and work to make a good one. We all need it.

Bibliography

Authors and titles referred to by Romesh Gunesekera

A House for Mr Biswas by V. S. Naipaul
À la recherche du temps perdu by Marcel Proust
A Portrait of the Artist as a Young Man by James Joyce
Anna Karenina by Leo Tolstoy
As You Like It by William Shakespeare
Death of a Salesman by Arthur Miller
Don Quixote by Miguel de Cervantes
The Enigma of Arrival by V. S. Naipaul
Essays of Three Decades by Thomas Mann
Far From the Madding Crowd by Thomas Hardy
Frankenstein by Mary Shelley
How to Become a Novelist by Dorothea Brande.
Howl by Allen Ginsberg
Huckleberry Finn by Mark Twain
Jane Eyre by Charlotte Brontë
King Lear by William Shakespeare
Lectures on Literature by Vladimir Nabokov
Madame Bovary by Gustave Flaubert
Midnight's Children by Salman Rushdie
Moby Dick by Herman Melville
Monkfish Moon by Romesh Gunesekera
On the Road by Jack Kerouac
Pride and Prejudice by Jane Austen
Reef by Romesh Gunesekera
Shorter Oxford Dictionary
The Day of the Jackal by Frederick Forsyth

The English Patient by Michael Ondaatje
The God of Small Things by Arundhati Roy
The Great Gatsby by F. Scott Fitzgerald
To the Lighthouse by Virginia Woolf
Tristram Shandy by Laurence Sterne
War and Peace by Leo Tolstoy
Wuthering Heights by Emily Brontë

Authors and titles referred to by A. L. Kennedy

A Million Little Pieces by James Frey
Canada by Richard Ford
Handcarved Coffins by Truman Capote
Justine by Marquis de Sade
King Lear by William Shakespeare
Memoirs of the Twentieth Century by Samuel Madden
Umbrella by Will Self
The Writer's Handbook
The Writers' and Artists' Yearbook

Other writers referred to

William S. Burroughs, Brion Gysin, Zane Grey, Alastair MacLean, Ian Fleming, Leslie Charteris, Chinua Achebe, C. L. R. James, W. B. Yeats, Fyodor Dostoyevsky, Daniel Defoe, Ernest Hemingway, Anton Chekhov, Samuel Beckett, Gertrude Stein, Charles Dickens, Émile Zola, Upton Sinclair, Aleksandr Solzhenitsyn, Ivan Klima, Samuel Beckett, William Faulkner, E. M. Forster, Gabriel Garcia Márquez, Milan Kundera, Don DeLillo, Johann Wolfgang von Goethe, Edgar Alan Poe, Arthur Conan Doyle, J. D. Salinger, Muriel Spark, Graham Greene, Anthony Trollope, Flannery O'Connor, Samuel Johnson, W. Somerset Maugham, C. S. Lewis, Robert Louis Stevenson, Alan Sillitoe, John Steinbeck, João Ubaldo Ribeiro and Juan Perucho.

In addition there are other books listed in the resources section and by the guest contributors.

Index